KING OF X

KING OF

THE TRUE STORY OF AN ECSTASY EMPIRE

CHRISTOPHER KING

ISBNs: 978-1-7356963-0-0 (pbk); 978-1-7356963-1-7 (ebook)

Cover design by Daymon Warren
Book design by Mayfly Design

First Printing: 2020
Printed in the United States of America

CONTENTS

KING OF X

CHAPTER 1

GROWING UP

I was born and raised in Dallas, Texas. Naturally, I'll always be an avid Dallas Cowboys fan. My mom would tell me as a kid that if you really want something to happen all you have to do is pray about it. So, I prayed every night: "God, please let the Dallas Cowboys win the Super Bowl," and wouldn't you know it, that year Roger Staubach led them to their first Super Bowl victory. I thought to myself, *this is really going to be an easy life because this praying really works.*

Of course, I would find out later that it's not that easy. Maybe I should try it again now and pray for Dak and Zeke?. My dad owned a chain of restaurants. Several in Dallas, one in Denton, Texas where he went to college, and several others in Nashville, Tennessee and Atlanta, Georgia. I remember him first closing the restaurants in Dallas, then the one in Denton, and then moving us to Atlanta. Then closing the restaurant there and moving us to the last one in Nashville. When the final restaurant closed in Nashville we moved to a small town in Ruston, Louisiana. We went from always living in a nice home to living in a mobile home. I remember first seeing it. It was old with several of the windows broken out. My grandfather owned a tractor parts supply company in Dallas. My dads' new plan was to sell tractor supplies to dealerships throughout the Midwest for my grandfather.

When that didn't work out, my dad soon got into the oil business as a Wildcatter and once he discovered and re-drilled an old oil field back in Texas, investor money started coming and it wasn't long before we were living in a big house on the hill in

Ruston Louisiana. Then, after several years of success, things began going wrong for my dad in the oil business. Soon we were broke again and Dad decided to move the family back to Dallas. I remember a framed picture of my dad when he was going to college at North Texas. It was an article in a Dallas newspaper about how he had worked at the Ford plant in Dallas and at the same time put himself through business college at North Texas. As a kid growing up, the only thing that I could see was my dad working hard at everything. But in the end, never having anything to show for it. I remember thinking to myself, *if that's the way life is, I don't want any part of it.* So, as a teenager I vowed to find some way to strike it rich someday so I wouldn't have to work hard every day of my life with no guarantee of having anything to show for it in the end. When we had money, everything at home seemed to be great, but when we were broke life at home was miserable. So, I was brought up in an environment where I believed money was the key to happiness. In my mind, I believed that I could do anything that I wanted to without putting too much effort into it.

As a Sophomore in high school I was bored with it, so I decided to drop out, and take my G.E.D. I passed all of my entry exams for college and entered into Louisiana Tech University the same year. Soon afterward, Dad moved the family back to Dallas, and it didn't take long before he was striking it rich again. I somehow thought it would be different this time around for my family. I decided to transfer to the same college my dad went to just outside Dallas at the University of North Texas. I ended up meeting a girl at a local night club in Dallas. Her name was Kiersten and she was also a student at North Texas. Everything seemed to be going well. Dad was successful in his new business, I was in college, and I had a good-looking girlfriend, too.

CHAPTER 2

THE COLLEGE SCENE

Having the hot girlfriend and going to college seemed like the perfect life. But it didn't take long for me to realize that you can't just get by in college and make it. It was starting to become clear to me now, I didn't know as much as I thought I knew. Everything that I thought I wouldn't need from high school was becoming just the opposite. After two years of struggling with my grades I realized it was time for me to make a change. This was the same town where my dad had opened his first restaurant when he was in college. I borrowed the money from my grandmother to open my first restaurant and persuaded Dad and my younger brother Justin to come help me set it up. I decided to name it after my brother.

So, here I am 21 years old with my first business. Justin's Restaurant in Denton, Texas. Everything that my dad taught me about the charbroiled hamburger business was paying off. We sold four dollar pitchers of beer to bring in the college crowd, but it was the food that kept them coming back. I mean, we were as close to the campus as you could possibly be, and with the smoke from the hamburgers wafting out of the kitchen, you could smell the food from miles away. It didn't take long for Justin's to become the most popular hangout on campus.

With my newfound success I thought I was King of the World! (No pun intended). If you've never been to Texas, let me remind you that the Lone Star State has some of the most beautiful women in the world. With the University of North Texas only 30 minutes away from Dallas, I had never seen so many beautiful girls in my life! In the evenings, Justin's became more of a bar atmosphere than a restaurant. It was by far the most popular hangout on campus. Eventually, it became so crazy at night that I had to hire a bouncer to keep the peace. He was a black guy named Robert who was an offensive lineman for the North Texas football team. He was so big that nobody messed with him. Actually, one guy tried, but I'll never forget that chump getting tossed over a car like a rag doll out front one night.

Life couldn't be better for me. Business was booming, and there was no shortage of hot girls to date. I was young, successful and having the time of my life.

Then one day everything began to change. This guy named Billy came in and asked me if I had ever tried a drug called Ecstasy. I told him that I had never done drugs before, and that I wasn't interested. He insisted that I take some with me and try them after work. With a shrug, I put them in my pocket and went home.

When I got home that night I decided to try one, and from that day on I was hooked. It was a feeling like I had never experienced before in my life. The next night I decided to invite this girl that I was seeing by the name of Lauri over after work and we both did Ecstasy together. This drug called Ecstasy made me feel like I was on top of the world! Everything felt great! Everything was incredible. We could stay up and listen to music, or talk. My girl was beautiful, sex was awesome and business was booming at the restaurant. It didn't matter what we did, when we were on this drug called Ecstasy, everything was fun.

Before long I was buying 10 or 20 units of Ecstasy from Billy every week. My girlfriend and I were having friends over several times a week for parties after work. Then the parties increased to the point where we were having them almost every night. These were the craziest and wildest parties imaginable. Ecstasy was known as "The Love Drug." Everyone was your best friend and happy in this euphoric world that we were now in.

Slowly but surely, I began to neglect my business because of my drug use. Especially in the restaurant business, you have to be there and prepare for each day or something will inevitably go wrong. And it did go wrong. Fast. Alcohol, food, and money began to disappear. I had nobody to blame but myself.

With the parties becoming more frequent and lasting all night, I began to find myself unable to work the next day. Sometimes we would open late or not at all. With Ecstasy costing $20 each, the profits from the restaurant began to dry up. In just a short time, I had gone from being a young, successful business owner, to a person who was now addicted to this drug called Ecstasy.

I tried to keep the restaurant going. In my mind I believed that I could keep it going and use Ecstasy at the same time. But the truth was that I had become more irresponsible and more addicted. Finally, after several years of success, I had run the business into the ground. With no operating capital, I was forced to close the doors. Everything that I had worked so hard for was now lost. All because of this drug called Ecstasy. I wasn't even looking for it. It had found me.

Shortly after losing my business, my girlfriend left me. I think she became increasingly scared that my life was now taking a different direction. You know what they say: "No money no Honey." I remember telling a friend that Billy was just a dealer charging $20 a unit, and whoever is supplying him must be making millions. Now that I had lost everything, I vowed to find the source and make the big money myself.

CHAPTER 3

THE MISSION

With my business now closed down, there was nothing left for me in Denton, Texas. Everything that I had worked for was gone. That would be the end of my college experience. Arguably, the best time in my life was now gone.

I knew Billy was getting his Ecstasy from someone in Dallas because I remembered him mentioning something about it one night. I decided to move to Dallas and I made it my mission to find out everything that I could about this drug called Ecstasy. I began frequenting the local clubs where it was obvious that everyone there was on Ecstasy. It was still a legal drug at this time. At one bar they would sell you a pencil for twenty dollars and give you a free hit of Ecstasy. That was their way of getting around the law. They could give it to you but they couldn't sell it to you. I met a lot of local, small-time dealers along the way but I never could get close to the main source.

I bounced around from a bunch of jobs supervising at several restaurants to support myself along the way. One of the guys that I worked with told me about a friend of his having these wild parties at his apartment on weekends where everybody was on Ecstasy all the time. He invited me to go to the party with him the next Friday. When we arrived at this guy's apartment that Friday night, the first thing you notice is people hanging out everywhere having a great time. If you've ever been around people when they're "rolling," a term people used when they were on "X," you can spot them right away. Maybe I was onto something here. The guy's name was Mark. He was a young dude who was laid back, cordial, but cautious about what he said at the same time. I wanted to ask him about everyone on Ecstasy, but I decided to be patient and wait until the time was right. I knew if I could just bide my time and befriend this guy that I could find the source.

So, I made it a point to come over and hang out with Mark. I became a regular at his parties and it didn't take long before he started telling me where he was getting his X. He told me this story about his brother going to school at the University of Texas, and finding the recipe for Ecstasy online. At this time it was still legal. However, he said the DEA had recently removed the recipe from being online since it was now becoming an epidemic of widespread use across the country. It turns out that his brother and another guy were making Ecstasy locally, but now that it was on the brink of becoming illegal they were warned to get out of the business fast. Mark worked for his brother in the lab and knew everything from top to bottom.

Mark and I discussed the details of Ecstasy more each day. Even though his brother wanted to get out of the business while he could, it seemed like Mark wanted to do something on his own. It wasn't long before he began talking to me about working for him. I would often ask myself, "Why would he need me if he could do everything on his own?" Nonetheless, since I had set out on a mission to find out everything I could about Ecstasy, I just went along with it all. He rented a small shop to work on cars as a front. It had an office upstairs. He began ordering chemicals from different companies. He would have them delivered by UPS to his friends' apartments. In those days you could go into a local lab supply store and buy all the glassware and lab equipment you wanted to with cash and walk right out the door, no questions asked. Anyway, it didn't take long before he had everything there in the office warehouse upstairs and he was ready to make a batch of Ecstasy.

Here I was watching this guy show me how to make Ecstasy from top to bottom. I always say, "be careful what you set out to find, because if you look hard enough you'll probably find it." He told me his brother always sold them for five dollars each to get rid of them quickly. I remembered a guy named Randy back in

Denton who had once told me if I could ever get him Ecstasy at a good price that he could move them for me.

Several days later when everything was finished, I set up a meeting with him and dropped off the Ecstasy. It only took him one day and he was back with all of the money. I knew how to make it and I was the one selling it. It became clear to me very soon why Mark had chosen to work with me. He wanted to teach me how to make it and sell it while he made his share without getting his hands dirty. And, at the same time he wanted to be in control of everything.

We worked together for several more months. Mark became very arrogant and cocky. The problem for him now was that I knew how to do everything on my own and I sold everything, too. So, who really was in control? I told him that I was getting out and we parted ways.

CHAPTER 4

THE START

Now that I was on my own it was now time to start making my own wave. The process was so easy that it could be done just about anywhere without any big set up or smell. $3,000 worth of chemicals was enough to make $250,000. I never had to meet anybody else. I would give everything to Randy and he would come back with the money. We had a nice thing going now, and very few people knew about us either. Best of all, I was back on top again financially. The thought of losing my restaurant didn't hurt as bad anymore with all of that money that was flowing in. How many 24 year olds do you know who always had at least $250,000 in cash sitting around? We were making so much money so fast that we could do whatever we wanted whenever we wanted to. The Ecstasy was there and gone so fast that most of the time we only had our own personal supply on us. The one thing that we always did have a lot of was cash. We used to say, "If hiding your money somewhere is the only problem we have, then that's a pretty good problem." I remembered not so many years back as a teenager telling myself that I would someday find a way to make it rich fast. Well, there I was, making more money than I could ever imagine. I thought I was the slickest guy in the world.

We only worked when we wanted to. We could work three days and have enough money to last the rest of the year if we wanted. And if there was any wind on the street of some Ecstasy, it was there and gone so fast that nobody knew where it was coming from. Randy and I were moving right along and having the time of our lives. We bought nice cars, motorcycles, and expensive clothes. But we always kept it under the $10,000 limit so we wouldn't draw attention to ourselves.

CHAPTER 5

FRIENDS & GIRLFRIENDS

With lots of money and time on our hands, Randy and I began inviting a few of his friends from Denton over to hang out and party with us. I never was much of a socializer. I always preferred to hang out with my girlfriend rather than a bunch of guys, but I just happened to be single at this time. Anyway, some of the friends that Randy introduced me to included Carl, who he went to High School with, Trace, whose mom owned a ranch outside Denton which hosted Corporate parties, and David who was a friend of his who went to college at North Texas. Even though they were just meeting me face to face for the first time, they all knew me because they were all making money down the line. Remember these three names because they will all come into play later. We had all the time in the world. It didn't matter if it was a normal workday because none of us had jobs. So, we didn't really have to keep up with what day it was. We could hit the clubs in Dallas anytime we wanted. We could stay out all night. There was a club called "The Starck Club" in downtown Dallas. Anyone and everyone who was into the party scene knew about "The Starck Club." You could easily tell that almost everyone there was on Ecstasy. There will never be another time like that, where people could run around freely and openly party in the club scene without any problems from the authorities.

Ecstasy was the new drug. This was a time like no other when it came to the club scene. Everyone was happy. The clubs were packed. The girls were beautiful, wild, and crazy. They wanted to dance, drink and X with you all night. If you had Ecstasy to offer, all the girls flocked to you. A guy could pretty much have his pick of any girl he wanted. And there were so many gorgeous ones it was like we were living in a really good dream. This was just the beginning of the new thing called "Raves." Raves were all-night parties. New clubs were popping up all over town. This new drug spurred the renovation of the old rundown area of downtown known as "Deep Ellum."

This was a time when Ecstasy was still fairly new to authorities. They knew about it but the Federal Government was still rushing to try and outlaw it. I remember going to the one bar that sold you the pencil for twenty dollars. Now, it seemed like all of the bars in Dallas were selling you something just to give you the complimentary hit of Ecstasy. That was their way around the law. Life was crazy for all of us. We became a close knit group. We hung out together, partied together, and never let anyone else know what we were into. Then before long we all started getting serious girlfriends. Randy had started dating a girl named Shelley.

Trace had a girlfriend named Darla. Carl was dating a girl named Brandy who he met while studying for his law degree at Texas A&M. And I was seeing a girl named Stephanie who I'd just met. Stephanie worked at the Fashion Market in downtown Dallas. She was damn good looking, sophisticated and obviously very fashionable. We really hit it off and after dating for several months we decided to move in together. I remember when I had asked her to move in with me and she began to cry. "What's wrong?" I asked.

"If my dad finds out that I'm moving in with you he's not going to be very happy with me." We ended up getting an apartment together at Valley Ranch. Valley Ranch was also the headquarters for the Dallas Cowboys, right down the street from our apartment. In fact, some of the Cowboys players lived in the same apartment complex.

CHAPTER 6

VALLEY RANCH

Our first place together was at an apartment complex called "The Enclave." It had probably the nicest apartments in Valley Ranch. Stephanie's good friend Amber worked in the office at "The Enclave." She was very attractive, but I remember she always dated some weird guys. We used to have parties at our place and Randy would bring his girlfriend Shelly with him. Amber brought some guy named Dave that she was dating to our party one night. We would leave a bowl full of Ecstasy on the coffee table and anyone at the party could take as much as they wanted to do while they were there. Randy told me he saw Dave take a handful of Ecstasy and put them in his pocket before leaving. I told Stephanie about it and we made it a point to keep an eye on this guy next time Amber brought him to one of our parties. The next time he came to our party we were all doing lines of cocaine all night. I remember Dave doing our cocaine all night and then right before leaving he pulls out his own bag of cocaine and puts a line out for everybody before leaving. The next day Stephanie told Amber about Dave doing everybody else's cocaine all night and then finally breaking his own out and offering everyone one line before leaving. Amber always listened to Stephanie's advice and that was the last time we ever saw Dave again.

I guess the reason that I'm mentioning the guys that Amber dated is because the next guy she brought to the party was one I will never forget. His name was Bill. We used to love for Bill to come over and hang out with us because he lied so much that he believed his own lies. I called him Lying Bill. Randy and I were

15

always laughing because Lying Bill was always digging in his ass. So one day I decided to ask him why he was always pulling his pants out of his ass. And he told Randy and me, "I'm going to tell you guys something that I've never told anybody before." We waited. Then he said, "I had hemorrhoids, so I went to the doctor and they started the procedure to cut them out with a laser. And the surgery hurt so bad that I never went back the next day to finish the surgery.

I never laughed so hard in my life, and I told him "So you're running around with a half of a lasered hemorrhoid hanging off your ass?"

"Yeah I am," he replied.

"Sorry I asked," I said.

Anyway, Lying Bill didn't last too long with Amber, but I'll never forget that guy.

Then there was Trace and his girlfriend Darla. Remember, Trace is the one whose Mom owned a ranch outside Denton where they hosted corporate parties. It was a Western setting at the ranch. It looked as if you were in a movie setting like "Pale Rider" with Clint Eastwood. They had a limousine that they used to drive clients to the corporate parties, but most of the time Trace would have his chauffer drive him and Darla around Dallas while they free based cocaine in the back. Whenever he would come around he always made me very nervous because he was so high on cocaine. He didn't care if anybody saw him with his pipe and torch in hand.

He wasn't like that when I had first met him. I could tell that he was starting to get out there. He was always slurring his words so badly that I could barely understand him. I remember one night we all went out to a club in Dallas called Mistral's and he was hanging out of the top of the moonroof of the limo with his pipe and torch in his hand. I remember telling myself "we need to start separating ourselves from Trace and his girlfriend before he brings us all down."

We used to have what we called "Capping Parties" where we would get together at our apartment and we would all sit around in a circle on the floor. Everyone had a plate of Ecstasy powder and we would put the powder into the gelatin capsules one at a time.

I went through my phases of different drugs. When I was tired of doing X, then I would switch to cocaine for a while. Then I would get tired of that and use Meth for a while. I started getting to the point where I would constantly look for new hiding places. Stephanie would always have stacks of Home Decor magazines that she liked to keep. I would hide my aluminum foil pieces that I smoked Meth on in her magazines and she would get so mad when she would find them. I had a pipe that I would smoke Meth out of, too. I remember her telling me that her mom would be coming to visit the next day so I had better not leave anything out. So that night I decided to hide everything really good. The only problem was the next morning she reminded me that her mom was on her way over and she asked me where I hid my pipe. I told her that I hid it but I couldn't remember where. When her mom shows up she sits down on the couch and grabs one of the Home Décor magazines to look at—and one of my aluminum foils falls out and onto the floor! Stephanie told her that she didn't know what it was and quickly threw it away. Then, later, after her mom left she yelled at me, "You dumbass!"

"What's wrong now?" I asked.

"Not only did one of your aluminum foils fall out of my magazine, but after that my mom wanted some ice cream. When my mom started scooping some ice cream, she notices something weird in the bottom of the pale. Guess what's in the bottom of the ice cream?" Stephanie asked, her eyes burning with anger.

"Oh yeah, now I remember where I hid my pipe," I replied.

Then it all started coming back to me. I had let the ice cream thaw out, dropped the pipe in the bottom, then poured the melted ice cream back into the pail before freezing it again.

Stephanie was more than a little angry to say the least. Hey, how was I to know my "mother-in-law" would want some ice cream. It probably would have done her some good. My hiding places were so good that I couldn't even find them but then my girl's mother stumbles across two of them the same day. Go figure!

There were several times when the fire alarm would go off in the apartment complex, and I would wake up, panic, and start flushing everything down the toilet thinking that the law was coming to kick my door in.

There were definitely some wild times at Valley Ranch, but we needed to find a house with a little more privacy. I felt like we were starting to stick out at the apartment complex. It was time for us to move on.

CHAPTER 7

THE COPPELL INCIDENT

Anyone who is from the Dallas area knows that Coppell is just a few miles away from Valley Ranch. We needed a house with more privacy and space than what the apartment offered. Literally right down the street from where we were in Valley Ranch was the perfect housing district just inside the city limits of Coppell. All of the homes looked the same. It reminded me of a housing division from the movie "Edward Scissorhands." The only difference between each home was the color. This was perfect for us because we very much wanted to just blend in. We sure as hell didn't want to stick out. Nothing fancy.

Once we moved in we decided to completely remodel the inside of the house. I had asked permission from the owner of the home and he was more than happy to get his home fully remodeled free of charge. But the house still looked the same on the outside, a carbon copy of every other home in the neighborhood. Nobody except the owner of the home knew how lavish it now was on the inside.

It was perfect for us. Carpet, kitchen cabinets, tile and everything else brand new. Besides, money was no object. We were in our own perfect little world now. Randy and Shelley would come over and hang out with us. We could hang out all night and party as much as we wanted. Sometimes I would forget what day of the week it was, and I would actually have to ask somebody. They always assumed I was joking.

We had one game room with the real Arcade games. Defender, Asteroids, and Pac-Man. There was enough space now that we didn't have to worry anymore about making too much noise and bothering the neighbors like in the apartments. We had a big backyard. We bought a St. Bernard puppy and named her Meagan. Life was pretty good for us at this time.

Remember my younger brother Justin, after whom I had named my restaurant? He was now in his Senior year at Liberty Christian High School in Denton, Texas. He was a star on the Varsity football team. But he was having trouble living at home just like myself when I was younger. He wanted to move in with Stephanie and I, so after okaying it with Stephanie we decided to let him stay with us. Besides, I didn't have to subject him to what Randy and I were doing because we very rarely had to do anything. I mean we only had to work three or four days out of every year. I was driving a new 300ZX and Stephanie was driving a BMW. My brother needed something to drive to school so I bought him a Suzuki Samurai Jeep. After purchasing the new Jeep I decided to drive it for a few days and test it out before giving it to him.

One day I drove it to Randy's house in Denton to hang out at his place. Trace was there with his limo out front and as usual he was carrying his pipe and torch with him. He was even worse now than the last time that I saw him.

The next day Randy, Shelley, Stephanie and I are all hanging out when someone knocks at the door. I open the door to see Trace there with his pipe and torch and his chauffer standing out at his limo in the street. Not exactly what you want if you're trying to be low key in the neighborhood. I tell him to come in, that we need to have a little talk. "Don't ever come to my house again with that pipe and torch," I say. "I don't want the neighbors seeing that shit."

He could tell that I was serious so he went back to the limo and gave his pipe and torch to his chauffer. He came back inside and talked to Randy and I before leaving. Afterward, I told Randy that this guy would bring us down if we continued to let him come around and Randy agreed with me. Trace was the pure definition of a "loose cannon". Ready to explode at any time. There's no way that one could run around the Dallas area in a limousine smoking cocaine all the time and never get busted. My first thought at that point was that maybe he had already been busted and now he was an informant for the law. If so, that would explain why he didn't care.

Several days later I get a phone call from Trace and he's mumbling his words as usual. I could barely understand him. But I did hear him say something about a lot of busts going down in the Dallas area, so don't have anything in your house. Then he hangs up. Was he telling me in a roundabout way that he had snitched on me?

Remember the Suzuki Jeep that I had bought for my brother to drive to school? Remember that I had decided to drive it myself for the last week. I had decided to let my brother start driving it to school the following day. The next morning came and my brother took off to school in his Jeep. He stops on his way to school to pick up his friend Rowdy. They both had big duffle bags in the back seat with their football equipment inside. As soon as they pull into the school parking lot and park they're immediately surrounded by undercover cars with lights flashing. Then guys with guns drawn surround the Jeep and say, "Chris, you and your friend get out and get on the ground now."

My brother's first words were, "Hey, Rowdy, did you piss somebody off?"

"No, I didn't make anybody mad," he says.

Then they pull them out of the Jeep and throw them to the ground. Right there in front of all of his High School friends to see. Then one of the undercover agents puts a gun to my brother's head and says, "Chris, do you have the Ecstasy in those duffle bags?"

At that point my brother knew what was up. They had mistaken him for me because I had been driving the Jeep for the last week. Once they realized that they had made a mistake they couldn't just let them go because they knew they would call and tip me off. So they took my brother and Rowdy to their headquarters for questioning. I'll never forget the phone call that I get with somebody saying, "Hey, this is a friend from your brother's high school, and I just saw everything that happened. They pulled guns on your brother and Rowdy at the school and then took them away in undercover police car," and then the kid hung up.

I never to this day knew who that was. My sister Carren was visiting us at the time. So it was myself, Stephanie, and Carren in the house. I will say this, after just several minutes of that phone call I didn't have anything incriminating in my home. I did have some laboratory equipment and glassware in boxes but I wasn't willing to destroy them. I assumed I could not get in trouble for just that. I ran to the window in my brother's room because from there you could see in the distance the convenience store called Stop-n-Go. I could see a pickup truck backed in at the store with his parking lights on. I went to grab the binoculars from my room and returned to the window. When I looked again, this time with the binoculars I could see a guy looking straight at me with his own binoculars.

I told the girls that we were being watched and they both really started to panic. I told them to get in the car and start driving somewhere, and that I would call them when it was safe. After they left I began double checking the house for anything I shouldn't have. An hour passed and the guy was still sitting there in the truck at the convenience store, still staring at me with his binoculars. I decided it was time for me to make a move instead of waiting for them to come to me. I walked out the back door and headed straight in their direction. As soon as I made it to the parking lot I could see the guy in the truck start driving towards me. At the same instant that the truck reached me this Corvette slid in right behind me and they both jump out with guns drawn on me. "Get on the car now!" one of them shouted.

"We know that you have Ecstasy in that house," another guy said. I couldn't see their faces because they were both wearing black hoodies.

"I don't know what you're talking about," I told them.

"That's okay we'll find out what's in there soon enough," he said. It turned out they were waiting for a search warrant to be signed by a judge before they could enter the house. They brought me back to the house and the girls were just getting there too, brought by other undercover agents also wearing black hoodies. The girls were crying and scared and I told them not to worry, that everything will be okay.

When the police entered the house they were in awe of how lavish it was inside. This was the North Texas Narcotics Task Force, and now their boss walked in. You could tell this guy was serious business. Not only did he remind me of Tommy Lee Jones in the movie "The Fugitive," but his name was Don Jones. I had some glassware and some miscellaneous items in a box and they began asking me about them. He asked the undercover agents that worked for him, "Do you know who this guy is?"

"No, sir," one replied.

"Well, he's the kingpin of Ecstasy," their boss told them.

He then explained to me that he was not going to take me to jail at this time but that one of his agents was going to write out a confession for me to sign, and then he left. They were trying to make me sign something because they knew that they had nothing on me. After he left, one of the agents wrote out a confession and set it on the kitchen counter. But the agents were more interested in seeing what they could confiscate than they were getting a signed confession from me. They loaded up all of my arcade games along my big screen television and then they left. They forgot all about the confession that they wanted me to sign and left it sitting right there on the kitchen counter.

The next day I contacted my attorney and informed him about everything that had happened. He couldn't believe that they had forgotten the confession and told me to never sign anything. But he warned that I could still be in some trouble for the glassware that I had in my house. We decided that the best thing to do would be to leave town for a while.

CHAPTER 8

VEGAS

We decided we would move to Las Vegas. Why not? It would be a nice getaway where there's plenty to do. We loaded up a U-Haul with everything we had including our St. Bernard and hit the highway. All the way across the desert in a U-Haul with a huge St. Bernard puppy with us was a long journey. When we first drove into Las Vegas my first thought was "Wow, how did somebody decide to build a city out here in the middle of nowhere?"

Anyway, we found a nice apartment to rent and we settled into our new life in Vegas. We had a decent amount of money to last us for a while, but not enough to continue the lifestyle to which we had become accustomed. The biggest thing about Vegas that I would find out is that you need money and lots of it. Especially if you like to bet on sports like I do. We started going out at night gambling, drinking, and going to shows. You know, doing all the things that you're supposed to do in Vegas.

All this time I was staying in touch with my attorney back in Dallas to see if any charges would be coming. When you have plenty of money in Vegas, everything was great but when it started to get low everything started to sour really fast. I guess you could say it's that way just about anywhere when you don't have money. After several months in Vegas it was obvious that I would have to return to Dallas soon. I was down to about 10,000 dollars and my attorney was now informing me that they had come with an offer. I had the choice of taking six months in jail or two years of proba-tion. I decided to take the two years of probation instead of prison time.

We began packing everything and preparing for our return to Dallas. There was a lady who owned a ranch outside Las Vegas where she ran a boarding house for dogs. We kept Meagan there because we weren't allowed to keep her at the apartment. The lady had fallen in love with Meagan and had constantly told us if we ever wanted to find another home for her that she would be interested. We always told her no because we really loved the dog. But in the end, as hard as it was, we decided to give her up to the lady. On this lady's ranch she would have plenty of room to run and play, and we knew she would be well taken care of. With all of the uncertainties back in Dallas we knew she needed a home where she would be safe. It was very hard and I remember Stephanie crying. It was like giving one of your family members away. After telling the lady and Meagan goodbye we began our return to Dallas.

CHAPTER 9

THE RETURN

Now that we were back in Dallas it was time for me to meet with my attorney to accept my two year probation agreement. Remember, when you're on probation it's mandatory that you stay out of trouble. I was certain that I could stay out of trouble. As long as I could avoid jail time I didn't care. My attorney informed me that they would be returning my arcade games, big screen TV, and everything else they had taken from my home since they had no confession from me. He was certain that Don Jones would be there for my court date, and that he probably wasn't going to be all that happy to see me.

Sure enough, when we arrived at the courtroom, Don Jones was sitting all by himself right in the middle of the front row. My attorney and I took a seat directly behind him. I remember Don Jones taking a look directly over his left shoulder, then directly over his right. My attorney and I glanced at each other because we both knew who he was looking for. Then he turned around and said to me, "Good morning, Chris, nice to see you here today."

Once the proceedings were over my attorney and I began leaving the courtroom. As we were just about to leave I could see Don Jones heading in our direction. He walked up to me and said, "Chris, you got away from me this time, but we will meet again soon, and I will get you next time."

Without saying anything to him my attorney and I left the court. That guy left a lasting impression on me. This guy was the real life "Tommy Lee Jones."

CHAPTER 10

THE PARTY AT DENTON

Now that the probation problem was out of the way, we had to decide what to do next. Stephanie's brother Allen lived in Houston and ran a mobile upholstery repair business that serviced car dealerships. Stephanie wanted to move to Houston so she could work for her brother. Shortly after, I decided to move there with her also. But I quickly grew bored there with little or no money. After several months in Houston I told her that I needed to go back to Dallas to check on some things. I also told her about our friend David (a college student back in Denton that I had met through Randy) who was having a big party at his apartment this Saturday night. Stephanie reminded me that Randy and I had better not be anywhere around that party because Don Jones might be keeping an eye out on everybody you guys know, and you never know, he just might show up there. I told her not to worry, that we won't go to the party.

When I returned to Dallas, I decided to drive up to Randy's and hang out that Saturday. I told Randy about Stephanie saying that we should stay away from the party, that there would be a lot of people partying there all night, and that there was a possibility that Don Jones could show up for a raid. Randy and I were doing some cocaine at his house that night. Randy said, "Hey, let's go to the party for a while and see what's up." I put the coke in my pocket and just like that we were off to the party. When we got to the party there were people everywhere, inside and outside. The music was very loud and cars were parked everywhere. When we made it inside, Randy and I went with David in his room to do a line of coke with him. After several minutes of talking they wanted to go back into the living room to join the party. I told David to let me use the phone in his room to call Stephanie.

After they had left the room this bad feeling started to come over me. This was more than just a paranoid feeling from doing coke. This was a sudden gut feeling that the law was on their way. I went into the bathroom and pulled the roll of toilet paper off of the roller. I pulled the cardboard roller inside the roll inward, stuck the bag of coke inside, straightened up the cardboard, and then put the roll of toilet paper back on the roller before returning to use the phone. I sat down on the bed and began calling Stephanie. As soon as I could say hello, she was already saying to me "you're at the party aren't you?" Literally at the same time I was telling her "yes I'm at the party" I could hear a "boom" and a bunch of loud voices in the other room. "Down, everybody on the floor, hands behind your back!" I heard. Then they kicked the door in into the bedroom and undercover agents with black masks on confronted me with guns drawn. "Get down now, hands behind your back," they ordered.

I never even had a chance to say anything else to Stephanie. I just dropped the phone and did what I was told. I was certain that these were the same guys who were at my home in Coppell. With everybody handcuffed and on the ground the process began with everyone being searched. If you didn't have anything on you, you were free to go. If you had drugs on you or had a warrant you were escorted directly to jail. I'm not sure exactly how many people went to jail but there were quite a few.

While all of these undercover agents were standing over me, guess who walked in? None other than Don Jones himself. "Hello, Chris, I told you we would meet again," he said. "Did you check him?"

"Yes, he's clean, sir," the agent replied to him.

"Check the room and see what we find," Jones said.

While several of the agents were rummaging through everything in the room, Don Jones asked one of the agents, "Do you know who this guy is?"

The agent replied, "No, sir."

"Well, this is Chris King. The kingpin of Ecstasy," he said. All of the agents stopped searching for a moment to stare at me while still wearing their black masks. After searching for a little bit longer one of the agents said, "Sir, there's nothing here."

"Ok, Mr. King, you're free to go," Don Jones said. "But remember, I'm going to get you one of these days."

They let Randy and I go, and when we got back to his house there were already some of the guys waiting for us there. One of the guys said, "Chris, they let you go? I was certain they were going to get you with that coke."

"Hey, you have to be quick to catch a jackrabbit," I retorted.

Then Randy said, "Hey, you had that coke in your pocket. How did you get out of that? I was certain that they would get you."

"It's still there," I told him. "Let's go back and get it."

"Are you freaking crazy, they're probably still there," Randy said.

"No, they're gone, they were there to try and get me, I'm sure of that," I said. "And they would never suspect that I would come right back."

So, we drove back to David's apartment, got the coke, and returned to Randy's to hang out all night.

The next day I returned to Houston.

CHAPTER 11

THAT GUT FEELING

U p to this time Ecstasy was relatively unknown to authorities. It was still legal but authorities realized that they had an epidemic on their hands. Popularity was beginning to spread across the country, and new laws were quickly implemented to make all designer drugs illegal in the U.S. The reason for making the law for all designer drugs was because one could simply interchange one chemical with another. In other words, you could use Ethylamine Hydrochloride instead of Methylamine Hydrochloride thus making it MDEA or Eve instead of MDMA or Ecstasy. The chemists were finding ways to change it just a little bit in order to make it legal faster than the D.E.A. could change the law. So, finally they decided to ban any and all designer drugs.

Back in Dallas there were two guys that Randy and I knew named Frank and Blair. We had met them through some friends. These guys were known around the Dallas area for bringing in Ecstasy from California. They were both big guys. You could tell they pumped iron and did steroids. Randy would joke around and say, "the hell with Hanz and Franz." They had heard through the grapevine that Randy and I were supplying Ecstasy, and they were always trying to muscle their way in with us. We always told them some bullshit story and blew them off. They kept sending me a message that they had access to any chemicals if we wanted to do business with them.

I always sent a message that I would get back to them later. You know that old cliché about always go with your gut feeling? I was getting that gut feeling that something wasn't right about their offer. Remember what I'm telling you about following your gut feeling because this will come into play the rest of my story.

Now that procuring chemicals was no longer an option I considered taking a chance with these guys. I made a crucial mistake. I decided to go ahead with a deal with these guys out of desperation. I set up a meeting with Blair in Dallas. We ended up meeting at a Denny's parking lot. There were some signs that I should have noticed right away that I didn't think about until later that should have warned me that this might not be a good deal. Blair gets out of his car and gets into my car and we start talking. He says that he has the chemicals in his trunk and for me to come get them. When he opens his trunk he says "there they are" and for me to grab them. Why didn't he hand them to me or help me carry them? Then he tells me that he has a trailer on some friend's land out in Kaufman County where we can make the Ecstasy. If that's the case, why didn't we just meet there instead of in a highly visible parking lot at a Denny's restaurant?

I guess that I was so desperate to start making money that I didn't pick up on obvious "red flags." I took the chemicals with me and we set up a time to meet at the trailer out in the country the next day. The next evening I drove out there. It was off the main road and the entire area looked mysterious and weird. The place looked as though nobody had been there but it had electricity? This place gave me the creeps. I was getting that gut feeling about this entire deal. And the way that Blair was acting as though he was always in a hurry and never touching anything or helping me in any way.

After I got everything running I told Blair that I would meet him there again the next morning. When I got back to my apartment I told Stephanie that something didn't feel right about the entire deal. " Something isn't right," I said. "I don't feel good about going back tomorrow to check on everything," I say.

"You're just being paranoid," she told me.

"No, I have that gut feeling that something isn't right," I insisted.

"Well, you do what you want to, but I think you're just being paranoid," Stephanie said.

The next morning I took off to check it out even though I didn't feel good about it. When I got there, Blair was nowhere in sight. I decided to go ahead and check on it without him so I could get the hell out of here.

As soon as I was inside I began to get that gut feeling that I needed to get the hell out of there. I checked on everything and I was literally out of there in five minutes. It was the same gut feeling that I had when I was at the party in Denton. It was not a good feeling to have. Anyway, I jumped in my car and pulled out onto the main two-lane country road.

As soon as I pulled onto the main road, on both sides of the road as far as I could see, undercover police cars were lined up everywhere. That's not how you want to start your day off! No sooner had I pulled onto the main road, they all swung into position like a train in front of me and behind me. There must have been at least 40 undercover cars with all of them turning their lights on at the same time. They blocked me in both directions, then they got out and drew guns on me and told me to get out.

"This is the D.E.A. You're under arrest for the manufacture of a controlled substance." Then they read me my rights and placed me in the back of one of the undercover cars. A free ride straight to Mansfield Correctional Facility. My new home away from home with no Get Out of Jail Free pass.

I never had been to jail before. This would seemingly be the end of my Ecstasy life that I knew. Now the story starts to really get crazy.

CHAPTER 12

THE PEOPLE WE MEET

After they processed me and gave me my new bright orange jumpsuit, they stuck me in a holding cell with seven other inmates. This was the first time I had ever been in jail and it wasn't a very pleasant experience. Freezing cold air, crappy food, and a variety of different guys all crammed into an eight-man holding cell. My attorney had warned me not to speak to anyone about my case because there were snitches inside who get paid to befriend you and find out everything they can about your case. Then they can have even more evidence on you when you go to court. He also told me that I would have to stay in jail for two to three weeks until he could hopefully get a bond set for me. In the meantime, all that I could do was sit and wait.

There was this weird looking guy with a weird accent in the cell with us. He was from Germany and he even looked like Adolph Hitler. Everyone called him Doc. He spent most of his time talking to each inmate about their case. He would ask them what they were in for and then give them advice on what they should do. I thought to myself, "Maybe this is the snitch that my attorney was warning me about." He seemed more interested in giving advice than prying into details about what each person had done. But nevertheless, who knows?

"Hi, I'm Doctor Friedhelm Koenig, nice to meet you," he said with a weird German accent.

"What did they get you for?" he asked.

"I'm here for manufacturing Ecstasy," I told him.

His eyes grew big and he said, "Wow, I never met anyone who knew how to make Ecstasy." Then he asked, "Is it hard to make?"

"No, not if you have the chemicals," I replied.

"There must not be that many people making it," he said.

"No, I don't think so," I agreed.

"Ok, nice to meet you, we can talk more later," he concluded.

Later, I started asking the other inmates about this guy. They all told me the same thing about Doc. That he is so smart that everyone asks him for advice on their case.

My attorney came to see me and I told him about this German guy and he warned me not to talk to him because he might be a snitch. The next day Doc came and sat at my table again and started asking me about the chemicals used to make Ecstasy. Then he started asking me what I planned to do about my case. He advised me that I was looking at about five years in Federal Prison. Then he told me, "Hey, why don't you jump your bond and meet me in Mexico and we'll really get these mothafockas for putting us in here?" All of this in a crazy German accent.

"All you have to do is hide out for about six weeks until I get out of here," he said.

"Let me think about it and we'll talk more about it tomorrow," I told him.

Later that day my attorney came to see me. He told me that my bond should be set in about one week. I informed him about what this Doc guy was proposing and he warned me again not to talk to him or agree to anything because he might be a snitch. I went back to my bunk, laid down and started thinking about everything. Here we go, right back to that "gut feeling" moment again. I knew my gut feeling was right but I ignored it on the deal with Blair and that landed me directly here in jail. I had to be right this time or I could be in even more trouble. My "gut feeling" this time was telling me that this Doc guy wasn't bullshitting. But what if I'm wrong about this guy? I had only known him for a little over week and we were already talking about me running from the law and making Ecstasy together when we get out! If I'm wrong I won't be getting out in another week. But if I'm right and we both somehow could make it to Mexico then the sky was the limit! I had made a promise to myself that from now on I would always go with my "gut feeling" no matter what after not listening to myself on the deal with Blair.

I wasn't expecting to have to put the "gut feeling" theory to the test less than two weeks after getting busted but here I was facing another crucial decision. Nevertheless, my gut feeling was telling me that this guy was serious. I discarded the warning from my attorney and the next morning I sat down with Doc and told him, "Let's do this." We exchanged some phone numbers and mailing addresses where we could stay in touch. Several days later my attorney informed me that my bond was set. It was an all cash $5,000 bond which meant that if I didn't show up for court in two weeks that I would lose the $5,000. The next morning as I was leaving, Doc said, "I'll see you in about six weeks."

CHAPTER 13

ON THE RUN

When Stephanie picked me up from jail she said, "No more illegal stuff, right? You should do whatever time they give you and when you get out you should get a normal job like everybody else and forget about Ecstasy."

"Get ready, I'm going to jump my bond and we're going to Mexico where we can be free and make lots of money," I retorted.

"Are you crazy!" she exclaimed.

"Yeah, I guess I am," I said.

We knew now that our days together would be numbered. There was no way we could stay together once I took off on the run. Those two weeks together passed quickly and just like that here I was a fugitive on the run from the law. I had no plan of who I would stay with or where I would go. I only knew that I had to elude the law. All of this on the hope of meeting up with some crazy German who I only knew for several weeks and who was still in jail. I must be crazy, I thought to myself. We knew they would be coming to our apartment in Houston anytime now that I didn't show up for court back in Dallas. That gut feeling was back again and I knew it was time to go. The funny thing was that I had nowhere to go. So, the next morning I had Stephanie drop me off at the bus station and I headed back of all places towards Dallas.

Here I was on this bus from Houston to Dallas. Of course I was under an assumed name but nevertheless I was on my way back into the eye of the storm, straight back to Dallas with nowhere to go. And now I was a wanted fugitive. This wasn't a very bright spot in my life to say the least. I remember finding out later that the U.S. Marshals had stormed our apartment in Houston looking for me. Stephanie was very scared obviously. So much in fact that she packed her belongings and moved to Oklahoma City to work for her parents. My gut feeling was spot on. They had arrived the very next day looking for me. I was just one day ahead of them.

I remember my bus ride from Houston to Dallas. There's a big sign that says 'Huntsville State Prison, Exit 1 mile ahead.' I kept having this vision or premonition that they would just pull over and take me straight to prison right where that sign was. My options were limited to say the least. I didn't have that many friends and the few that I had were sure to be watched.

I decided to go to my grandmother's for a few days. I knew that I couldn't stay long. I started getting that gut feeling. I knew it was time to go. I told my grandmother that I had to leave. I could tell that she was worried about me, so I assured her not to worry and that I would be ok.

I didn't know that would be the last time that I would ever see her again. She was a great person and I will never forget her. Once again I would find out later that the U.S. Marshals would show up there the next day looking for me.

With nowhere to go I just started walking. I remember sleeping under a bridge for several nights. I had a little money and a few clothes in my backpack. How many times could I barely get away from the law? I remember reading the statistics about how the Marshals catch 9 out of every 10 fugitives within the first 30 days. I can believe that because they literally check every possibility where one could be. I had just been lucky so far. Maybe because I didn't know where I was going, then obviously they didn't know either.

This new life of being a fugitive was definitely no fun. Stephanie had a payphone where she would go to and I would call her at a certain time every day . I told her that I had nowhere else to go and that I needed to come hide at her new apartment in Oklahoma City. The next day she picked me up at the bus station. I ended up staying there for almost two weeks which was crazy. I knew that they would find her new address and be here anytime. Guess what? Here comes that gut feeling again. I told Stephanie that I need to leave.

Here I go on a bus again from OKC thru Dallas and back to Houston again. Guess what? The next day they showed up at Stephanie's apartment and searched the place for me. She told them that she'd had enough and wanted to get away. They warned her that they would be back to check again and gave her a number to call if she heard from me. I think since that one time I didn't follow my gut feeling on the deal with Blair that anytime I felt that feeling just a little I was gone. That was the only thing keeping me barely one step ahead of the authorities. How many times could I just keep riding the bus back and forth before I would get caught? I think they felt like sooner or later I would make a mistake and then they would catch me. That's probably how they catch most people.

I remember thinking, "I sure hope Doc gets out of jail soon." Here I go passing that Huntsville State Prison sign again. And once again I'm having this premonition about the bus stopping there and the authorities taking me straight to prison. Granted, it was a State Prison and where I would be going would be a Federal Prison if they catch me but it was always a simple reminder every time I passed that sign of just how much trouble I was in now. I only knew this one guy in Houston named Glen.

He was some guy that Randy knew through a friend of his named Brent who lived in Houston that could get him cocaine whenever he was in town. Not exactly the kind of guy I should be looking for, but when you're on the run and have no other options it doesn't really matter. I had his number and I had only met him one time. When I got to Houston I ended up walking all the way from the downtown bus station to some mall where I found a payphone to call this guy. He answered the phone and I told him who I was and that I was at this mall and he agreed to come pick me up. When he got there I decided to tell him my whole situation. I explained to him that I needed a place to stay for now and that if he could help me I would make sure he was compensated when I got back on my feet again. He told me about this friend of his who was a cocaine dealer and maybe I could stay at his place for a few days. And just like that, we were off to some cocaine dealer's apartment.

CHAPTER 14

HOUSTON, WE HAVE A PROBLEM

When we get to this guy's apartment Glen knocked at the door but there came no answer. Glen knocked again and someone said, "It's unlocked, come in." When we entered the apartment it was very dark inside and across the room you could barely see a guy sitting in a chair facing us with a shotgun in his hand. "What the hell are you doing, Rick?" Glenn said.

"Come in and shut the door," the guy replied. He never took his eyes off the front door, even once we are inside. This guy was a big time tweaker.

"Rick, give me that shotgun, you're going to hurt somebody" Glenn said.

"Who's this guy with you?" Rick asked with suspicion.

"He's a friend of mine," Glenn said. "He needs a place to stay and we came by to see if he could rent a room from you for several days."

"How do I know he's not the law?" Rick asked.

"He's not the law," Glenn promised.

"Ok, if he's not the law then let's all do a line of cocaine together," Rick challenged. So we all sat down at the table together and we all snorted a line of cocaine together. "Ok, you can have that back room for a few days," Rick offered. "Besides, I need somebody to keep an eye on the place for me when I go to the strip clubs at night," he added. Honestly, I think this guy just needed some-body to talk to.

This wasn't what I would call an ideal situation for a wanted fugitive staying at a tweaked out coke dealer's place. But it was better than staying on the street. Like they say, "beggars can't be choosers." Glenn left and told me that if I needed anything to give him a call.

"Hey, come watch this movie. Have you ever seen this movie before?" Rick said.

I came and sat down to see what movie he was watching. Guess what it was? "The Fugitive" with Tommy Lee Jones! Not exactly the movie I wanted to be watching at the moment, but I sat down to view it anyway. I swear, every time I saw a movie on somewhere it was always playing "The Fugitive." It's like I was living this dream about Don Jones always chasing me.

The only problem was that every day I woke up to the same nightmare. It wasn't a dream. Every night I would always walk to a payphone and call Stephanie at the payphone in OKC. She told me that she still hadn't heard anything from Doc, maybe he will never call and maybe I should just turn myself in, she urged.

"No, I have to keep buying more time," I insisted.

It was really crazy staying at Rick's place. There were some Mexicans who would come by every few days and drop off a kilo of cocaine. Then people would come by at all hours of the night to buy it.

I think Rick used more of his own stuff than he sold. Remember the saying, "don't get high on your own supply?" Maybe Rick needed to be watching "Scarface" instead of "The Fugitive." All that it would take for me to get caught here would be some tweaker leading the authorities here. Rick would take off for the strip clubs at night and leave me there to keep an eye on his place. That was fine with me because I didn't need to be going very many places anyway. He had his cocaine stashed in his room somewhere. I guess he was always concerned about someone breaking in while he was gone and stealing his stash.

If I got caught here I would be in even more trouble. The last place a wanted fugitive would need to get caught would be an apartment with a kilo of coke stashed inside. Most of the time I would just sit there by myself and watch television. It was always in the back of my mind that the authorities might check this place out sooner or later because they could check phone records of any of my friends to see if any of those numbers could be where I was staying. Since Randy and his friend Brent had called this number before, maybe they would eventually check it out I thought to myself. It wouldn't be that hard for them to work their way down the list of numbers called.

I remember it was a Friday night and as usual Rick had gone out to the strip clubs. I was sitting there as usual by myself when the phone rang. "Hey, how's it going? This is a friend of Rick's, is he home now?" someone asked.

"No, he's not in right now, he's gone out for a while," I replied. I knew right away who it was but I had to be calm and say the right words.

"Who am I speaking to?" he said.

"This is Eric his roommate," I replied.

"Ok, is there anyone else there right now?" the guy said.

"No, I'm the only one here," I answered.

"Ok, thank you, have a good evening," he said before hanging up.

At this point my blood pressure shot through the roof! For all I knew they could be sitting outside or either on their way to check out the place! I knew I had to leave now. I didn't have to sit around and wait for my gut feeling to kick in on this one. I stuffed my belongings in my backpack and headed out the door. If they were outside I was sure they would get me right away but I had to take a chance and walk. I was certain that they might stop by and check the spot sooner or later. It seemed as though I had walked forever before reaching a payphone. It was late at night with weird people riding by and hanging out everywhere.

I gave Glenn a call and told him to come pick me up, and to give Rick a call and let him know about the phone call so he can get his stuff out of there just in case the law is coming. I told Glenn that

I needed another place to stay. He informed me that he had this other friend who was a recovering alcoholic who might let me stay there and help him with his rent since he hadn't been working. I thought to myself "Ok, from a cocaine dealer to a recovering alcoholic. What do I have to lose?"

CHAPTER 15

WOLFMAN JOE AND THE BICYCLE

When we got to this guy's apartment this short little Mexican with scraggly looking hair and a beard answered the door. He had a bottle in his hand and he was obviously drunk. The place looked like a dump. Trash and dirty dishes were strewn everywhere. I remembered a famous Mexican named Wolfman Jack. This guy reminded me of him, so I named him Wolfman Joe. Glenn introduced us and asked if I could stay for a while, and that I could help him with his rent. He said, "Yeah, you can stay here as long as you help me with the rent and make some runs to the liquor store for me."

"Ok, you have a deal," I said.

It turns out that Wolfman Joe was on probation for his 13th DUI. The last DUI he had he crashed his car into some parked vehicles and was passed out in the car when the police arrived on the scene. In order for him to stay out of jail he was supposed to be going to rehab several times a week. But he wasn't going at all. He was paying another person in the class to sign his name for him every week. I'm not sure how long that would last before the police would come looking for him.

Just outside Wolfman Joe's apartment were some Coke machines and a newspaper stand. One night he told me to hold the door open for him and he started carrying the newspaper stand into his apartment.

It had a big concrete block as the base of it so it was fairly heavy. He turned it upside down and shook all of the change out of it. Then he took the stand back outside and said, "That's how you drink for free every day."

It was times like this when I would think to myself that maybe I should just turn myself in. I still had no word from Doc, and I was beginning to second guess my decision to run. I had to continue and try to hold out with the hope that I would hear from him soon. Wolfman Joe asked me if I could make a run to the liquor store for him. "There's my bike on the patio if you want to take it," he offered.

"Sure, why not?" I said.

When I get to the first stop sign there was a girl standing there. She said, "Hi, how are you doing? Can I get a ride with you?"

I guess it caught me off guard that someone would ask me that, so I didn't really know what to say. "Sure, come get on," I said. She climbed on and it didn't take me very long to realize that this wasn't going to work. My knees were hitting the handlebars as I tried to peddle. I pulled over and said, "Hey, I'm sorry but this isn't going to work."

"Ok, thanks for the ride anyway," she said.

When I returned from the liquor store I told Wolfman Joe about what happened and he died laughing. I didn't think it was that funny. The next day I decided to walk and look for a job because I needed money. There was a strip club about three miles from the apartment. I decided to go inside and see about a job. When I entered there were nice looking girls everywhere. I asked one of the girls if they were hiring and she said, "Yes, follow me." She took me to an office in the back.

There was this little Italian guy there sitting at his desk while this good looking girl was dancing on his desk. He said, "Hello, I'm Jay. Have a seat," and the girl got off of his desk. "We'll finish this interview later," he told her.

"Sorry about that, I was doing an interview. I love my job," he said. "What brings you here?" he asked.

"I need a job," I told him.

"I have a barback position. It's cash only, would you be interested?"

"Sure, it sounds good, thanks.".

"Ok," he said, "you can start tomorrow."

When I got back to Wolfman Joe's I tell him that I got a job and he said, "Good, I won't have to get money out of the newspaper stand anymore. But I already got the money out of there tonight."

"Can you make a run to the liquor store for me?" he asked.

"Sure, why not," I replied.

The only problem was that it had started to rain. On the way out the door Wolfman Joe admonished, "Hey, don't pick up any girls on the bike today," as he was laughing.

"I'll try not to," I quipped.

"Let's see what kind of story you come back with today," he chided.

I took off and it started raining even harder. Anyone who's ever been in Houston knows how hard it rains. After I purchased the six-pack of beer I tied the plastic bag to the front handlebars so I could ride back. The roads were too full with water so I had to get up on the sidewalk to ride back. As I was riding up onto the sidewalk the plastic bag that was holding the beer broke. It fell into the front tire and locked the front end up sending me and the beer flying over the handlebars and into a grassy area flooded with mud and water. I remember just sitting there all wet in a puddle of water with beers scattered everywhere. As people were riding by I remember them honking and laughing out the window at me. I thought to myself, "What the hell am I doing?" Surely it couldn't get any worse than this. So I was thinking, "What the hell, I might as well sit here and drink a beer."

When I picked up one of the beers from the water I couldn't tell until it was too late that there was a pinhole in the side of the can and as I went to open it the beer shoots me right in the eye. More people rode by honking and laughing at me. "Yeah, I guess that it could get worse," I thought to myself.

When I finally got back to the apartment and told Wolfman

Joe what had happened he fell off the couch because he was laughing so hard. I couldn't really believe what bad luck I was having myself.

The next night I went to work at the strip club. It was perfect for me because I was able to have cash every night, and the girls were nice to look at of course. The next day Wolfman Joe asked me to make another run to the beer store for him. I think he was just as interested in seeing what would happen to me on the bike as he was getting alcohol. "To hell with that bike," I said.

"Come on, surely nothing can happen three times in a row," he challenged. So, I took off again to the liquor store and I went inside and purchase a six-pack of beer. When I came out of the store, guess what? Somebody had stolen the freaking bike! Once again I couldn't believe my bad luck. With no other choice, I walked all the way back from the liquor store.

When I got back to the apartment Wolfman Joe asked, "What took you so long this time?"

"You're not going to believe this," I said. "Someone stole the freaking bike while I was in the liquor store."

I never saw anyone laugh so hard in my life. Once again I didn't think it was that funny, but I had to laugh also about what crazy misfortune I was having in my life. Could my life get any worse than it was for me at this time? Probably not.

In the meantime, Stephanie had received a letter from Doc that he wasn't getting out anytime soon. It was encouraging that he had made contact but he didn't know when he would be out. That meant that he would still be there even longer. And I would have to stay on the run even longer. How long could I continue to elude the authorities? Had I made the wrong decision to run? Would my luck eventually run out? All of these questions constantly ran through my mind.

CHAPTER 16

STRIP CLUB ICICLES

I continued with my job at the strip club. There were always lots of guys coming in with plenty of money to burn. Sometimes I would reminisce about the days when I had $250,000 at my disposal to do anything I wanted to do. Now my life had been reduced to being a barback fugitive with a longshot dream of making it big again.

Jay was a crazy boss. He always had some new hot girl dancing for him on his desk. The same words always came out of his mouth. "I love my job."

I remember it was a Friday night at work and all of a sudden the law burst in through the front door. I was working behind the bar when agents with black jackets with gold letters on the back stormed into the building. It was hectic everywhere. Girls were scattering and screaming at the same time. I thought to myself, "They're here to get me." I eased out from behind the bar and started walking through the back hallway towards the back door. Just as I reached the back door someone opened it from the outside and reporters from the local news, cameras following them, rushed inside. They were coming straight towards me. There was a freezer door to my right. I grabbed the clipboard off of the wall just before they reached me. I opened the door, dashed inside and slammed the door shut behind me.

The freezer was very loud from the air blowing inside, making it hard for me to hear what was going on. It was freezing cold inside the cooler. All that I could hope for was that nobody opened the door and looked in here. I tried to put my ear up against the cooler wall to listen but it was so cold that my ear would stick to it. The only sounds that I could hear were people arguing or yelling through the hallway that exited the back door. Probably the girls that were being escorted out the back door to jail for whatever reason was my guess.

I never had felt so cold in my life. My hands and face were frozen to the point where I couldn't feel anything. I checked my watch and I had been in the freezer for over two hours. I didn't know how much longer I could stay in there without freezing to death. But as long as there was still noise in the hallway I had to stay in there. Finally, after about two hours of freezing in the cooler I couldn't hear any more noise.

I was so frozen that I could barely walk. My clipboard was frozen to the shelves so I yanked it loose. I had to come out of there now and hope for the best. When I opened the door there was nobody in the hallway. I walked around to the bar where there now was only one person sitting there. It was my boss Jay.

"Where have you been?" he asked.

"I was in the freezer taking inventory," I replied.

He had a grin on his face and I asked him, "What's so funny?"

"You have icicles hanging off of your eyebrows," he said. "How long were you in there?"

"I'm not sure."

I think he knew that I was probably hiding in there but he never said anything else about it. "What happened?" I asked.

"It was the ATF," he told me. "They had been sending undercover agents in here to see if the girls were following proper procedures about lewd dancing. They're not supposed to make contact with the customers when they are dancing," he explained.

"Where is everybody else?" I asked.

"Most of the girls went to jail for lewd dancing and anyone who had a warrant out for them also went to jail. Even the bartender went to jail for unpaid traffic tickets," he said. "I think you're the only one here that they didn't check. Everybody else went to jail. They ran everybody's name who works here. I was certain that you were gone too.

Then he told me that there probably wouldn't be any work for three or four weeks while the investigation was going on. "Ok, I'll stay in touch with you to see when there is work again," I said.

On my way home I was thinking to myself, 'how can that happen where almost everyone at the club goes to jail except a wanted fugitive hiding in the freezer?" Maybe I really did have nine lives.

CHAPTER 17

JUST 1 FISH

Now that the strip club was shut down money was hard to come by. Wolfman Joe still liked to drink every day but didn't work. He started bringing the newspaper rack back inside at night to shake the change out of it so he could have money to drink. There was no more money for me to pay the electric bill, so it got shut off. It was wintertime and it was cold outside. Wolfman Joe had run an extension cord through the dryer vent that ran outside behind the Coke machines. He used that extension cord to plug in a light inside the apartment. We had no way to heat the place so we would fire up the grill from the patio inside the apartment just to stay warm. We were eating cold hot dogs with bread and that was about it.

When I called Stephanie that night she gave me a number to get in touch with Randy because he was supposed to be in Houston this coming weekend. I gave him a call and he asked, "Have you thought about turning yourself in?"

"I think about it all of the time, but it's too late for me to turn back now," I told him.

He then told me he's coming to Houston this weekend and we set up a place to meet. When he got to Houston, Randy told me he was in town to pick up something to take back to Denton with him.

I had already spoken to Stephanie and told her that I was out of options again. She informed me that the U.S. Marshals had not been by in a while to see if I would show up there. It was closing in on four months for me being on the run now. It was supposed to only be six weeks but that didn't happen. It seemed like 10 years at this point.

I told Randy that I needed to get to OKC and stay there. "Are you crazy?" he said. "They will be looking there for you again. Are you sure that you don't want to just turn yourself in?"

"Quit asking me if I want to turn myself in," I said. "I'm in it until the end now."

"Ok, I'm driving back to Denton tonight. Do you want to ride with me and have Stephanie pick you up?" he asked.

"Yeah, that sounds good," I replied.

I called Stephanie and let her know the time and place to pick me up in Denton, but to get there I would have to drive past that Huntsville State Prison sign again and straight through Dallas. Remember, Denton, Texas was Don Jones territory. I sure didn't want to stay around there very long. We went to Carl's place in Houston to grab his belongings. I hung out with Carl and we talked about everything. He also asked me if I wanted to turn myself in.

"Hey, I'm tired of everybody asking me that," I said.

In the meantime, Randy had gone out to his car to put his belongings in there and hide whatever dope he was bringing back with him. At the time I wasn't sure what it was or where he had hidden it. I really didn't care. All I wanted was to get to OKC. He came back inside and asked, "Are you ready?"

"It's 1:00 in the morning, don't you think that it would be better if we drove later in the morning when there's more traffic on the road?" I suggested.

"No, we'll be fine, let's go," he replied.

So, we took off from Houston heading right back towards Dallas. It seemed like all I was ever doing was going back and forth on the same highway from Houston to Dallas all the time. As we were leaving Houston I started getting that same premonition like I always did about that Huntsville State Prison sign that I always passed by. It was late at night and we were practically the only car on the highway. I didn't have any identification on me and I knew that if we were to get pulled over that they would probably finally catch me. I decided to come up with some kind of backup story just in case. Randy had the radio blasting to Guns-n-Roses so I wasn't sure if he was even listening to me.

I remembered there was a quarterback named Bobby Hebert that used to play for the New Orleans Saints. I decided to use the name Chris Hebert from Louisiana in case we got pulled over. I began telling Randy that if we get pulled over my name is Chris Hebert from Louisiana and that we have been fishing in Galveston with our friend Carl. And if they ask how did we do fishing you tell them that you and Carl caught all of the fish but that I caught just one fish.

"Yeah, that sounds like a good story," Randy agreed.

I was thinking to myself that this guy isn't listening to anything that I'm saying, especially with the music so loud. The closer that we got to Huntsville the more I kept thinking about that damn prison sign. Maybe it was just a constant reminder every time I would pass it that I could be going to jail soon. For whatever reason I was getting more and more nervous by the minute. Then as we started getting really close I began to get that gut feeling that something bad was getting ready to happen. As soon as we reached the next sign that said Huntsville State Prison Next Exit, I saw a car pass us going the other direction on the highway. As it passed, I could see that it was a Texas Highway Patrol car. As he passed I took a look back and saw him hitting his brake lights and making a U-turn in the middle of the highway.

I told Randy, "I was right all along, he's turning around to come get us."

I could see that Randy was no longer relaxed and enjoying his music anymore. We were both nervous! Guess where he pulled us over? Right in front of the Huntsville State Prison sign! Just as I had seen in my mind over and over again. He stepped out of his car and walked up to Randy's window. Randy rolled down his window and the Trooper looked in at both of us and said, "How are you guys doing? You guys are out traveling the roads late tonight," he said. "Do you guys have any identification on you."

Randy handed him his driver's license and I told him that I don't have any identification on me. "Ok, what's your name?" he asked.

"Chris Hebert, sir," I replied.

"And where are you from, Chris Hebert?" he asked.

"I'm from Louisiana, sir," I told him.

"Ok, you guys wait here," he said.

He went back and got in his patrol car to run our names. I told Randy to just relax and not to look nervous. It's very hard to be so nervous inside but not show it on the outside, but that's what we had to try and do. All kinds of things were messing with my mind now. All of those premonitions in my mind about getting stopped by this sign. And here I was living it out. I was living a bad dream. Potentially a nightmare.

The sign was right in front of me and the Trooper was running my name. He came to my side of the car and said, "Sir, can you step to the back of the car please?"

"Yes, sir," I replied. I stepped out of the car and headed to the back.

"I ran your name and nothing came back with your name, probably because you are from Louisiana," he said. He had the trunk open now and he asked me to step over to the side a little bit. He wanted to keep an eye on me as he began his search in the trunk. The first thing that he did was to pick up Randy's boots. He took a quick look at them and threw them back in the trunk as he continued his search. He started pulling up the lining to see if there was anything underneath. "So, Chris, you're from Louisiana?" he stated. "What brings you to this neck of the woods?"

"Randy and I and our friend Carl all went fishing in Galveston yesterday," I told him.

"Wait here, I'll be back," he said. He returned to Randy's window to start questioning him but I couldn't hear what they were saying. I could only hope that Randy had remembered the entire story that I had come up with. Any discrepancies from either one of us meant that we were both going to jail. When he returned to the back of the car he started searching through the trunk again.

"So you guys went fishing?" he said.

"Yes, sir," I answered.

"So how did you do fishing?" he asked.

"They caught all of the fish, I caught just one fish," I said. As soon as he heard that he shut the trunk and said, "Ok, you guys have a safe trip back and be careful traveling this late at night."

"Ok, thank you, sir," I said and just like that we were back on the road again. He followed behind us for a while. I told Randy whatever you do, don't speed. The trooper eventually made a U-turn and went the other direction on the highway. We were both still shaking for quite some time after that close encounter. I asked Randy, "Where did you hide whatever it is that you are bringing back with you?"

"I hid it inside my boots," he said.

"Are you kidding me, that was the first place that he looked was inside your boots," I retorted.

"I put it in the most obvious spot because nobody would ever take the time to look in the most obvious spot," he said.

I guess the trooper was convinced of our story once we both had told him that I had caught just one fish. He probably thought that there was nobody crazy enough to make up a story like that.

CHAPTER 18

THE CALL

Now that I was in OKC with Stephanie I knew that I was really taking a chance. For the first three months the Marshals had come by every few days to see if I was there. Now I was closing in on five months on the run. I couldn't be staying in a more dangerous place. Somehow I was still free, if that's what you want to call it. I knew that it would be just a matter of time before they would return here looking for me.

Stephanie's parents also owned an auto upholstery repair business in OKC just like her brother's business in Houston. We would go to the local car dealerships to repair cigarette burns in the cars. I liked to go with her and help. Besides, I didn't want to be a sitting duck in case the law showed up at her apartment. It was always a tense moment anytime we were coming or going from her place. I was a nervous wreck staying there. There was a loft upstairs that had an attic entrance. I always kept it ready to climb into just in case the law showed up. One Friday evening there was a knock at the front door. We were getting ready to go out and get something to eat. I had just taken a shower and put on clean clothes. But that didn't matter. I climbed up into the attic and hid.

I got all dusty and dirty only to find out that it was just a salesman trying to sell something.

Every day I was a nervous wreck. Now I was closing in on six months being on the run from the law. Doc had originally told me that he would be out in six weeks not six months. Stephanie was always telling me that I should just turn myself in, but she knew that I would never give up that easily. I have to admit that there were so many times that I considered it, but I always made the decision to keep running. I had come this far and narrowly escaped so many times. I couldn't just give up and say it was all for nothing now.

The only issue now was time. Father Time definitely was not on my side. How much longer could I stay here before they would come looking for me? One Saturday night Stephanie had to drive to Tulsa to see her parents. I stayed at her apartment by myself that night. After she left I decided to watch some television. I turned on the television and guess what movie was playing? You're right. Tommy Lee Jones in "The Fugitive." I was living a bad dream!

I knew that I shouldn't stay here in OKC much longer. Monday morning arrived and we headed out to the car dealerships to work. I told Stephanie that maybe she should put me on a bus back to Houston again soon before the law shows up at her apartment.

As soon as we started working, Stephanie's phone rang. "He's right here," she said and handed me the phone.

"Hello?" I said.

Then there was this weird German accent on the phone that I hadn't heard in six months saying, "Where are you, Mothafucka?"

"I'm in OKC," I told him.

"Get your ass on a plane and get to Tijuana," he replied. "Here's my address at the hotel where I'm staying, I'll be here when you get here, MothaFocka."

"I was wondering if I would ever hear from you," I said. "I'll leave tomorrow."

When I got off of the phone with Doc I told Stephanie that was the call that I had been waiting to get for six months. Now I just had to get to Mexico.

CHAPTER 19

THE FLIGHT

Traveling back in those days was a lot different than it is today. 9/11 changed everything. Back then, you could literally call up a travel agency and buy a ticket under any name. I had Stephanie purchase my ticket and after we picked it up she dropped me off at the airport. If I could get on the plane here with no problem, then I would only have one connecting flight in Denver to worry about.

I gave Stephanie a kiss good-bye and told her to wait for my call from Mexico to join me. I was able to walk straight through the airport, get my boarding pass and get on the plane with no problems. It was definitely a nervous walk through the airport. I didn't really know until I had made it on the plane if I would make it or not. Once the plane was in the air I felt a sense of relief, but I still had a long way to go. All I had was one more plane to catch from Denver to San Diego. When we landed in Denver I knew this would probably be the last big obstacle for me. When I went to the ticket counter to get my boarding pass the lady asked me for some identification. I told her that I forgot to bring it with me and she said, "Sir, you don't have any identification at all?"

"No, ma'am I don't."

Then I said, "I forgot my wallet because I was running late to the airport."

She went over and began to talk to some old guy who was her supervisor as she was pointing at me. I'm thinking to myself that this can't be good. "What if I've come this far to only get caught at the last obstacle?" I thought to myself.

He walked over to me. "Sir, you don't have any identification?" he asked.

I told him the same story about forgetting my wallet. "We're normally not supposed to let anyone fly without any identification but since you did have a booked flight under your name from OKC and this is just a connecting flight, we'll make an exception this time, but next time you need to make sure you travel with some identification," he warned me.

"Yes, sir. Thank you," I said gratefully.

I began my walk to my final flight. After everything that I had gone through to get to this point, would I finally make it? It was the longest walk ever from the ticket counter to the boarding area. It felt as though every other person in the airport was either a policeman or an undercover agent staring at me. I told myself just to stay cool, that I was just being paranoid. They were already boarding when I got to the line. I showed the lady my boarding pass and just like that I was sitting on the plane looking out the window. The next thing I know we were in the air. "Maybe I'm going to make it after all," I thought to myself.

CHAPTER 20

FIRST IMPRESSIONS

I remember a good friend of mine had once told me that if he could live anywhere he wanted that he would love to live in San Diego, California. As soon as I grabbed a taxi and headed towards the border I could see what he was talking about. The city, coastline and the weather here are beautiful. I could see why so many people would want to live in such a spectacular place. I was nonetheless still very anxious to get across the border and see what this place called Tijuana, Mexico was all about.

This was my first time ever to San Diego and Tijuana. I was a long way from Texas now. The further that I could get from there the better I felt. The taxi driver dropped me off at the border and I began my walk across the border. As soon as I made it across into Mexico I thought to myself, "What the hell am I doing in a place like this?" People were coming from all directions trying to sell me something. I couldn't understand anything anyone was saying. There were donkeys on the corner painted like zebras where you could get your picture taken with them. There was trash everywhere and the homes on the tops of the hills looked as though they could fall off at any time. I gave the taxi driver a hotel address where Doc was staying and we headed in that direction. When we finally arrived at the hotel I paid the taxi driver and headed inside.

The hotel looked run down. I walked into the lobby and Doc was at the front counter checking out. He turned around and said, "What took you so long to get here, mothafokka? Grab those two duffle bags over there and wait for me outside while I pay this bill."

I wonder what's in these bags? I was thinking to myself. That's all I needed was to get in trouble with whatever is in these duffle bags on my first day in another country.

When we got in the taxi and headed towards another hotel I asked Doc what was in the duffle bags?

"They're the fire extinguishers from the hotel," he told me. "We need them for our laboratory and besides they were charging me too much money for my room, those mothafokkas," he said with his weird German accent.

This guy is crazier than me, I thought to myself.

CHAPTER 21

WINGING IT

We ended up getting some rooms at some cheap hotel on Calle Revolucion in downtown Tijuana. Anybody who has ever been to Tijuana knows that's where all the action is. There are bars and casinos everywhere. On the weekends there are people drinking and partying anywhere you go. I wasn't here for that, though. At least not yet. I had come a long way to get to this point. Now there was real work to do. Even though I was in another country in a crappy hotel room, it was somewhat of a relief to be here instead of being on the run back home.

Once the word got out to all of my guys, the money started coming in. The word was that we needed money and we needed it fast. Doc wasn't interested in a small warehouse. He wanted something big. I was used to just having a small garage to work in, but this guy had other ideas. I told Randy to find money anywhere possible. Carl was sending money and their friend Brent from Houston was also sending money. Even my old boss Jay from the strip club in Houston was sending money. He didn't even know what it was for but I told him that he would find out soon enough. Doc was also getting money from his contacts back in Germany. One day I told Doc, "Hey, it's nice to be working with a real chemist now."

He snapped, "Don't ever call me a chemist again, mothafokka, I'm a scientist and I can build rocket ships if I want to, mothafokka."

"Ok, chill the fuck out, dude," I said. Then I asked him what happens if we can't get any particular chemical that's on the DEA's precursor list.

He replied, "Don't worry, if I can't get it, then I'll just make that chemical. I'll start from dirt if I have to, mothafokka."

I never questioned his ability or expertise ever again.

It had been six months for me on the run and now we were closing in on living in a crappy motel for six more months in Mexico. We were both starting to feel as though it was now or never. We were close to our goal of just having a shot at it now. Doc finally found an 8,000 square foot warehouse, and the deal was closed several days later. One might think that it's easy to find a warehouse in Mexico, but with the new NAFTA agreement with the U.S. there were lots of new businesses popping up everywhere and warehouses were hard to find. When we went to close the deal on the warehouse the guy spoke pretty good English. He told Doc, "You speak such perfect Spanish. Where did you learn to speak Spanish so well?"

Doc replied, "I taught myself." No doubt true. When I had met Doc in jail he spoke six or seven languages already.

In the six months that he was still in jail he'd taught himself how to speak Spanish fluently. When we finished closing the deal on the warehouse he told me, "Can you believe that mothafokka asked me where did I learn Spanish. I taught myself, mothafokka."

I remember the last thing on our list that we needed was a car to transport everything that we had purchased to the warehouse. We needed a car with a big trunk, and the only one that we could find with a big enough trunk was a '77 gold Cadillac D'ville for which we paid $700. We were now at the point where it was now or never. There was no more money for a hotel and barely enough money for food.

CHAPTER 22

DE JA VU

Randy had come to Tijuana with the last money that we could possibly gather from everyone that we knew. It was myself, Doc, and Randy in an 8,000 square foot warehouse in the middle of a neighborhood in Tijuana. It was winter now and it seemed as though it was even colder inside this huge warehouse. We would run Randy's car or the old Cadillac just to stay warm or get some sleep. It was as though we were camping out inside this huge empty warehouse. The first run would be on me. We had enough chemicals to make approximately 10,000 units of Ecstasy. There was a bathroom with a shower but no hot water. Try taking a cold shower in a freezing cold warehouse in a foreign country. Although a freezing cold shower was better than no shower at all.

The warehouse was surrounded by homes on all sides. Some of the local hoodlums that hung out outside the warehouse began getting very curious about activity inside. I remember one night one of the guys off of the street had tried to look in through the front door as Doc was entering. He and Doc had some words and the next thing I knew Doc was chasing this guy out into the road. Doc grabbed him and threw him to the ground while punching him. I ran outside and pulled Doc off of the guy. "Doc, what's this all about ?" I said.

"This mothafokka pulled a knife on me and says he's going to rob me. Nobody's going to rob me, mothafokka!" Doc spat.

With this incident Doc had sent a message to the local hoodlums. That was the first and last time we ever had any problems with someone trying to rob us. In the meantime we were finally closing in on our first run. It had been a long time getting to this point. We ended up with around 9,000 units of Ecstasy. Randy took them with him and now all we could do was wait. We had to hope that everything would go down without any glitches. There was no more money and no more material or time. All that Doc and I could do now was anxiously await Randy's return.

Three days later Randy returned to the warehouse with $45,000. The word coming back from Houston was to send everything you can make. Doc's eyes lit up like a Christmas tree. "We'll see if they can handle everything that I can make, mothafokkas" he declared.

I was already thinking De Ja Vu all over again in my mind to the days when I used to have money and do whatever I wanted. The possibilities now were endless, but I didn't want to get ahead of myself. We still had a long way to go. There was still a lot of work to be done, but it was a start.

CHAPTER 23

RISE AGAIN

That was the last time that I would ever have any more hands on with the lab environment. With the money we had made we rented a condo right on the beach just outside Rosarito, Mexico. Rosarito is about a 20-minute drive down the coast from the U.S.-Mexico border, which is by the way the largest border crossing in the world. I kept some money to run on but I gave Doc the majority of the money to continue purchasing whatever he wanted for the lab. As the money continued to come in, Doc wanted more and more every day. Sometimes I would have to slow him down because he wanted to buy everything right away. With money he was like a kid in a candy store.

In the meantime, the money kept rolling in. Before long we were moving 15 to 20,000 units per week. Between $75,000 to $100,000 per week. The only major problem that we had was that we didn't have a pill press. We had to sit and encapsulate that many units into gelatin capsules every week. Nevertheless, life was pretty good for us now. Stephanie moved down as soon as we had money. Stephanie and I along with Randy and Shelley would all go down to the beach and hang out all day. Then we might all go to Rosarito and party all night. It didn't matter because we could do whatever we wanted to. But the majority of the money kept going to Doc.

Week by week that 8,000 square foot warehouse was being filled with the best of everything that money could buy for a lab. If I told you what it had looked like just six months after we had started you probably wouldn't believe me. From one end to the other there was something running as far as you could see down all the aisles. We had one huge glass custom-made beaker that stood over 10 feet tall with a thermal wrap that cost $70,000. Doc said that was custom-made to his specs and that it was the only one in the world.

The final big purchase that he made was for a pill press. This pill press cost close to $200,000 and was capable of producing 38,000 units per hour. In less than six months Doc had fully industrialized the entire process. I remember going to check out the new pill press and there was a representative there from the company who had sold it. He was there to show Doc how to calibrate and run the new press. He was actually using the Ecstasy powder to calibrate the press. "What if he tells somebody what the powder is?" I whispered to Doc.

"Don't worry, he doesn't know what the powder is, mothafokka," Doc replied.

When it was all said and done the total cost for the entire lab was around 1.2 million dollars. The purity of the Ecstasy was cleaner than anything ever.

It was so pure that Doc called it pharmaceutical grade. There was none more pure in the world. Doc's motto was, "If it's not white it's not right, mothafokka."

After six months of renting a condo together it was time for us to get our own places now. There was a new townhome and condo community on the beach just before you get to Puerto Nuevo. Puerto Nuevo is just past Rosarito and is a well-known tourist attraction that is renowned for their lobster and drinks. Doc ended up renting a condo on the 7th floor and Stephanie and I ended up renting a townhome. The townhome was perfect for me because it had a garage. You could take the service road after exiting the toll road and easily access my garage from there. After moving in to our new homes we spent around $75,000 on two new Ford Explorers.

Life was crazy for us at this time. The only thing that I ever really worried about was being wanted back in the U.S. That was always in the back of my mind. Eventually, my brother Justin joined us in Mexico. We needed more people to help with transportation in both directions. He brought his friend from high school Rowdy with him. Remember, Rowdy was his friend who was with my brother way back during the incident with the Narcotics Task Force back in Denton. They also brought another friend of theirs from Denton with them named James (Jimmy) Guy.

CHAPTER 24

THE WORLD IS YOURS

The business continued to grow. I needed a room where we could all hang out and handle daily operations. I was always paranoid about rooms with windows. So the master bathroom became the spot. We bought a money counter and set it up in the bathroom. We also installed a surveillance system that ran cameras from the bathroom to the front door, courtyard, and back door. Everything could be watched from the bathroom monitors. Tony Montana didn't have shit on us.

Sales climbed from 50,000 units per week to 100,000 units in just several months now that the pill press was in full operation. We always sold for 5.00 dollars a unit no matter what. Doc always received 3.00 dollars a unit and I would receive 2.00 a unit. That made Doc's cut $300,000 a week and mine $200,000 a week. Stephanie was always telling me that she wanted to take the first $1,000,000 dollars in cash and throw it on the bed and lay in the middle of it, so we did. Have you ever seen one million dollars in twenties thrown on a bed?

Life was crazy for all of us. There was never a dull moment. We were a very close-knit group that kept to ourselves. Randy and Shelley would come over often and hang out with us. Rowdy and Jimmy handled the transportation of Ecstasy into the U.S.

My brother Justin handled the money coming from San Diego to Mexico. We bought brand new sport bikes to go riding. We also wanted them just in case we ever needed to make a quick getaway. We would take the bikes for a ride on Friday nights into Rosarito and hang out at a bar called Papas & Beer. We liked to jump up on the toll road and wind the bikes up. It was like a mini Autobahn. I had a sport bike before so I knew how to ride. Jimmy was the craziest rider that we had ever seen. He would dart around an 18-wheeler in a place we called Dead Man's Curve and barely make it before oncoming traffic. We always told him to take it easy or he was going to kill himself someday. Justin was a pretty good rider also but none of us could ride like Jimmy. We never let Rowdy get a bike because he had a history of crashing almost every car that he ever had.

Stephanie always liked to go shopping in San Diego during the day while me and the guys were hanging out in the master bathroom most of the time. She would usually spend around $5,000 a week. Some days me and the guys would spend all day in the bathroom counting money and doing coke, or meth, and drinking. We would study the college and pro football games to bet on for the upcoming weekend.

All of the Caliente sports book locations knew us. And we knew where all of their locations were too. On Saturdays I would send Justin, Rowdy and Jimmy to three different Caliente locations to place $5,000 each on one game.($15,000 dollars for that game). Bro and I had always been pretty good at betting on football.

These times for all of us were so crazy. We were all having the time of our lives. Most of the time I would only see Doc about once a week when he would drop off the next shipment and pick up his money. One day we were in the store and he was in the candy section standing there eating candy. He put some candy in his pocket while smiling as he walked out of the store without paying. Even though he had several thousand dollars in his pocket. Then he would break out laughing and say, "I got those mothafokkas. He got a thrill out of stealing two dollars' worth of candy.

I had purchased one of the older Porsche 928's to restore but Doc had to outdo me by purchasing a new $90,000 Porsche 928 GTS. He had the Porsche and a new Mercedes but he never drove either one of them. He preferred to drive the old gold $700 Cadillac. I was driving down the toll road from Rosarito to Tijuana one day when I saw Doc pass me in the old Cadillac. There were two young guys that also passed in a small Volkswagen GTI.

They were pulling up next to Doc while taunting him and making gestures as they passed. As they passed me I remember thinking to myself that these guys don't know who they're messing with. As I was approaching the end of the toll road I could see as I got closer to the pay booths that there were police cars with their lights on surrounding the Volkswagen GTI. The same car with the young guys who were taunting Doc. As I passed by I said to myself, "What in the hell happened here?" The entire back end of the Volkswagen was crushed and there was no sign of Doc anywhere. When I arrived at the laboratory Doc was outside looking at the front end of the old Cadillac. Those old Cadillacs were made out of cast iron. Not even a scratch was on the front bumper. "Doc, what happened?" I asked.

They kept fucking with me so I got those mothafokkas," Doc explained. As soon as they had stopped in the back of the line, Doc had pulled up right behind them and intentionally rammed into the back of their car. Then he had backed up and paid at several booths over. I knew this guy was freaking crazy.

CHAPTER 25

THE EXPLOSION

Running a full-scale industrial style lab was no easy endeavor. Doc had hired a local guy named Gustavo to help with the daily tasks. Doc had trained him on how to run everything in the lab. Doc came by my house to tell me that he was going to Acapulco for the weekend, and that Gustavo would take care of everything at the lab while he was gone. It was a Saturday night and I was upstairs relaxing. I was going over the Sunday football games that I wanted to bet on when the doorbell rang. Stephanie was downstairs and went to the door. She came upstairs with a worried look on her face. "Gustavo is at the front door and something is wrong," she told me.

I dropped my newspaper and rushed to the front door. When I got there Gustavo was standing there completely covered in black soot. All you could see were his eyes, and he was in tears. "Everything is gone," he said.

"What do you mean everything is gone?" I asked.

"The lab, everything is gone," he said as he was crying. "Everything blew up! The entire lab is gone," he said.

"Come inside and sit down," I told him.

I tried several times to call Doc but I got no answer. "I can't even go back now because the fire department and the police are both there," he said.

"Ok, then go home and stay there until you here from myself or Doc," I instructed.

After Gustavo left I continued to try and call Doc all night but I got no answer. The next morning I decided to take a ride down to the lab and see what it looked like. I was just several blocks away from the lab and I could already tell that it was not going to be good. Up ahead I could see local news vans parked on the side of the road. The entire area before you get to the lab was blocked off with yellow tape. It was impossible to get a view from that angle so I decided to go around and up the hill to see it from the other street. Looking down the hill I could see everything. There must have been at least 100 of the local neighbors walking in a circle in front of the warehouse. They all had signs in their hands that said in Spanish that they didn't want this business in their neighborhood anymore. There were policemen, firemen, and news reporters everywhere. I backed out and left before anyone noticed me. According to the local news it was like a bomb going off. It had rocked an entire square block of the neighborhood.

Doc finally gave me a call later that day from Acapulco. I could tell by the tone of his voice that either the secretary or Gustavo had already informed him. Doc let me know that he would be back the next day to assess the damage and see what we can do.

It turned out that Gustavo had tried to cool down a beaker containing ether by placing it inside the refrigerator. The ether, which is very volatile, ended up igniting from the light bulb inside the refrigerator. When the refrigerator blew it was like a bomb going off. It went flying through the lab destroying everything in its path. The explosion was so strong that it had rocked every home in the neighborhood and could be heard from miles away. Gustavo was very lucky that it didn't kill him.

When Doc returned to Tijuana he began the process of paying off anybody that he had to. Somehow the $70,000 custom flask was unscathed and the pill press was good since it was upstairs. Total losses for the lab were around $600,000, plus another $200,000 in payouts. $800,000 dollars gone just like that!

It only took Doc several weeks to find a new warehouse. This warehouse was almost identical in size to the first one. When you have plenty of money to throw at something you can rebuild really fast. In less than 60 days Doc was up and running again as if nothing had ever happened.

CHAPTER 26

TOO MUCH OF A GOOD THING

The two months of downtime had actually pushed the demand even higher. Word was coming back to send more and send it fast. Within the first 30 days of starting up again, sales quickly surpassed 200,000 units per week. Now my income was $400,000 per week and Doc's was $600,000. Even at that rate I was finding it hard to keep up with Doc. He was running the lab full throttle now. He probably felt more of a sense of urgency after everything that had happened. I'm sure there was always someone that he was having to pay off.

The extra room off of my courtyard and garage was filled to the ceiling with large Rubbermaid containers full of Ecstasy. I would stay up late or all night sometime to coordinate everything. My meth use had increased and sometimes I would go into my own little world. Stephanie had mentioned something about wanting a pedestal with something sitting on top of it as you enter the condo. I told her that I wanted one with the wavy glass blocks built into the front of it. Since I was certain that I wouldn't be able to find one anywhere like that I decided to build it myself. When I used meth my mind would go way out there. I would start projects that never ended. I became obsessed with building this pedestal. It ended up turning into this crazy art project that grew more by the day.

My meth use had increased to the point where I was using every day. Every day I would come up with something new for this pedestal. I decided since the glass blocks were 12 inches by 12 inches that I would buy three 12 inch TV's and put one behind each glass block. I would have Stephanie bring me 12 inch televisions from San Diego when she went shopping. The only problem was that a 12 inch television is really 13 inches unless you take it out of the protective casing. Hence, three TV's stacked inside a pedestal behind the glass blocks with no protective covers.

Working with televisions that were no longer in their case was very dangerous, especially in the hands of someone using meth all night. Every time that I would break one or short it out trying to install it inside the pedestal I would just throw it away.12 inch televisions with audio/video hook ups were not cheap but I didn't care. Stephanie said that she was getting tired of buying TV's and that the neighbors were probably wondering why there were so many broken TV's in the trash all the time. I can't even count how many times I got shocked messing around with those TV's. But now I was on a good one and I was just getting started.

With money flowing in I started looking for new hiding places. Now my days and nights consisted of doing meth, counting and hiding money, and working on my art project.

I worked on the art project in the extra room upstairs. I had an extra surveillance camera and monitor installed for that room so I could keep an eye on anything outside while working on my art project. Every day I would come up with something new for this pedestal. What was supposed to be just a pedestal with wavy glass blocks built into it, went from that to having a TV behind each block. All of the TV's ran to a DVD player where the same music video would play on all three TV's at the same time. On the top of the pedestal I decided to build a hollow stucco lamp base with lit up designer marbles all the way around it. The lamp base had an n-scale train that ran through the front and around the back of the base through both sides. It had a flowing built-in river underneath the outside of the base and underneath the train with the riverfall in the front. All of this flowing water had to be sealed in really good. I couldn't afford to have the water leak down onto televisions that didn't have any casings. Then on top of the base was a paper mache planet that was lit up from inside .Everything was clear coated to give it a nice clear shine. I told you that I was on a good one now. I promise you there was no other art project like this in the world.

Tony Montana's globe in his house didn't have shit on this one. It grew so tall that I had to get the guys to help me move it downstairs to the living room where there were vaulted ceilings. After adding airplanes and rockets and all kinds of other things that were circling the planet, it took a ladder to reach the top. It was one of my favorite times of the year now because the Super Bowl was coming up. This year it was the 49ers and the Chargers. I went to the Caliente Sports Book in Rosarito and placed $50,000 on the 49ers. It turned out to be an easy win that paid $45,000. Several days after the Super Bowl, I returned to Caliente to collect my winnings. They told me that they didn't have $95,000 at that location. The dog track and sports book in Tijuana is also owned by Caliente. They ended up sending an armored truck from Caliente in Tijuana all the way to Rosarito just to deliver my money. When the armored truck arrived they brought the money to the counter and counted out $95,000 and I placed it inside my briefcase. The security guard asked me if I needed an escort to my car. "Sure, why not," I told him. I really didn't care about an escort but I just played along so that the security guard could get his tip. I gave him $200 just to walk to the car.

Sales continued to increase. We were hitting the 250,000 to 300,000 unit mark per week sometimes. On those weeks the increased sales jumped my profits to $600,000 per week and Doc's was $900,000 per week. Much of it went into real estate. I purchased my townhome that we were living in for $235,000. I paid for it with all twenty-dollar bills. The following week I decided to buy another home, also right on the beach for $350,000. I paid for this home with all one hundred-dollar bills. There was a realtor lady named Kathy who was brokering the deal for the second home. When I had purchased the townhome the cash deal was done with the owner of the property. No bank was needed for that transaction. But with the second home we would need to meet Kathy at the Banamex bank in Rosarito to close the deal. The night before the meeting Stephanie reminded me that Kathy had called to remind us that it was an all-cash deal. I was thinking to myself, "What better deal than a cash deal." The next day Stephanie came into the master bathroom and reminded me that the appointment was in one hour. I was on another good one all night and I told her not to worry, that I'd be ready. I jumped in the shower, got dressed and loaded $350,000 all in 100's into two briefcases. When we arrived at the bank in Rosarito I followed Stephanie inside with my two briefcases.

Kathy was waiting for us there and she had a weird look on her face. She and Stephanie had a quick conversation. Then Stephanie came over and whispered to me, "She said it was supposed to be an all-cash deal as in a cashier's check."

"Hey, you said it was an all-cash deal, this looks like cash to me," I said.

After Kathy spoke to a representative from the bank we followed them into a big room in the back of the bank where they brought out their money counter and set it on the table in front of us. I thought to myself, "My money counter looks nicer than theirs." I opened the briefcase and placed $350,000 in 100 dollar bills on the table. Once everything was counted I signed some paperwork and that was it. Now I had two beachfront properties within three miles of each other.

The next day I decided to go back to work on the art project. It was kind of stuffy inside the condo that day so I decided to move it out into the courtyard to work on it. It took myself, Justin and Rowdy to get it out there. I lifted one of the TV's out of the pedestal to work on it. I sat it on the ground until I could get to it. The only problem that I had now was that it had started to rain just a little. So we had to move everything back inside.

There's a reason why they sell TV's with a casing. A TV that has only wires and circuit boards even though it isn't plugged in will still shock the hell out of you. I had lost count of how many times I had shocked myself working on this crazy art project. I'm sure a little bit of drizzle from the rain coming down now wouldn't help things either. I asked Rowdy to pick up the TV and carry it inside for me. "It's not going to shock me is it?" he asked.

"No, it's not plugged in," I replied.

He went to pick it up and all you could hear was, "Oh shit, you fucker, that shocked the hell out of me!"

I fell to the ground because I was laughing so hard. It shocked him good enough to lose his footing. "That was some funny shit," I said.

"That shit wasn't funny!" he shouted.

It was starting to become a problem where to hide all of the cash flowing in every week. I began putting it inside the walls of the home. Then I reworked the bottom base of the cabinets in the master bathroom to where the base boards could be taken on or off at any time because I installed magnets on the backsides to keep them in place. Almost every imaginable place you could think of inside that home had cash hidden in it. I told you that I was on a good one.

I made copies of all my winning receipts from betting on football games at Caliente. I had collected close to $400,000 in winning tickets. If anyone ever asked me what I did for a living I would tell them that I'm a professional gambler. Not that it really mattered at this point but you never know when you might need an alibi.

CHAPTER 27

SPY GAMES

The Master bedroom was right where you could see the ocean from the large sliding glass windows at the back. One night when we were going to bed I kept seeing this weird red flash that kept hitting the back windows of the room. It was if someone was shining a laser on and off at the back of our home. It didn't happen all of the time but it was enough to get my attention. Every time that Stephanie and I would go out to eat or go shopping together in Rosarito we would come home and always get that feeling that someone had been inside our home. It always seemed like something wasn't in the exact position as it was before we left. There were millions of dollars' worth of Ecstasy and cash everywhere. I told Stephanie that I felt like somebody might be listening to our conversations when we are inside the house. I had her go to a store in San Diego called the Spy Factory and buy me a listening device detector. I knew if there indeed was something that it would be hidden somewhere around the master bathroom area since that's where we spent the majority of our time. As soon as I turned it on it detected something in the master bathroom. But it wouldn't stay on very long. It was as if they could remotely turn the listening device off as soon as I turned on the detector.

I told Stephanie to go for a walk on the beach with me. I needed to talk to her away from the house so I could tell her what my plan was. "I think somebody is listening to our conversations when we are in the house. This is what we're going to do. When we get back inside the house I want you to ask me to go shopping with you in San Diego tomorrow for some new pictures for the house. That way whoever is listening will think that we are both leaving the house together the next day. But I want you to go by yourself and I'll stay behind to see if anyone is trying to break in," I said.

After we returned to the Master bathroom and carried out our conversation, I got a phone call several minutes later from Randy. "Hey, how's it going, Randy," I said.

"It's going good, Shelley and I are sitting here thinking about going shopping in San Diego tomorrow. We're thinking about buying some pictures or art for our place down here," Randy said.

"Oh yeah, that's weird because Stephanie and I were just talking about doing the same thing tomorrow," I told him. When I got off of the phone I wrote down what Randy just said to me on a piece of paper and handed it to Stephanie. Now we both were true believers that our home was bugged. The next morning we followed through with our plan.

"Are you ready to go?" Stephanie asked.

"Yeah, I'm ready, let's go," I replied.

She went into the garage, got into the car and left. I laid down in the bathtub and didn't make a sound. Remember, I had the surveillance monitors set up in the master bathroom so I could hear a pin drop anywhere outside the house. It only took about ten minutes after she left when I heard something on the monitor at the back sliding glass door downstairs. I jumped out of the bathtub and immediately I could see some guy on the monitor trying to break in downstairs. I ran downstairs as fast as I could but by the time I arrived to the back door and unlocked it he was gone. I couldn't get a good enough look at him to tell who he was.

Now I knew that I was right all along. Somebody had been getting in our home or at least trying to. All of this set me into full defense mode. I had a really good idea who was the main person trying to listen in on my conversations and I had just the right plan to flush him out. If they want to listen to everything that I say then I would give them plenty to listen to. Later that night when Stephanie came into the master bathroom to talk to me I asked her, "Hey, do you remember that party in Denton that you told me not to go to at David's?"

"I thought Shelley was Randy's girlfriend, but I know that she slept with David after the party that night," I said.

"How do you know?" Stephanie asked.

"Because David told me that they had slept together," I said.

"That's messed up," Stephanie declared.

Now the bait was set, so all I had to do now was wait.

The next night Randy called me and told me that he and Shelley were coming over to visit us. When they arrived we all sat down at the table in the dining room. Randy and I were the only ones who were talking. Shelley just sat there with her arms crossed and didn't say a word. "What's wrong with Shelley? Is she in a bad mood," I asked.

"No, she's not feeling well today," Randy claimed.

She had a look on her face like she wanted to kill somebody. When they left, she didn't even say goodbye. Now what could make her so mad that she didn't even want to say goodbye? I told you I would give them an earful!

The next night Randy came over by himself. "Where is Shelley?" I asked.

"I got tired of her shit and I sent her home," Randy said. Just like that I had my answer. Randy had all the money he wanted from everything. We even went way back to the days when it was just the two of us making Ecstasy in the garage together.

But once you lose my trust it's a done deal. I can never trust you again.

About a week later Randy called me and wanted to come over and visit again. Shelley was back. I guess they made up? I had gone upstairs to the bedroom. I can't remember what for, but we had the blinds open upstairs and downstairs to see the ocean view that day. As I entered the bedroom I caught a glimpse of that red flashing light again that I had been seeing off of the back window. When I ran to the window I could see out back that there was a palm tree where something was attached to the side of it and it was aiming a laser directly at the back sliding glass door off of the master bedroom patio. "Hey, there's something on the side of that tree shooting a red laser at our home," I said to Stephanie.

I ran downstairs to go and see what it was, but by the time I got downstairs Randy had already left out the back door and was gone around the corner of the complex. I went to take a look at the palm tree but whatever was there was already gone. There was a piece of bark dangling from the side of the tree as if something had been ripped off of the side. I ran back inside and Shelley was still sitting at the table with a conspicuous look on her face.

"Where's Randy?" I asked.

"I think he went outside to smoke," Shelley said.

"He went out the back door and around the corner to smoke?" It didn't make sense.

When I go out the front door I see Randy walking toward me from his truck. "What are you doing?" I asked.

"I was getting a cigarette out of my truck," he said. He was acting nervous. "We have to go, I have some things I need to take care of, I'll talk to you later," he told me.

He and Shelley got in his truck and they left. That was the last time they would ever come to my house again. I started doing my own investigation into what the red laser could be that was on the palm tree. It turns out that the same company where I purchased my bugging detector also sold a laser device that bounces infrared signals off of glass to a distant location where conversations could be heard. That explained why I couldn't find anything inside my home, because it wasn't inside it was outside.

CHAPTER 28

GREED

Doc continued to produce more and more Ecstasy. With my organization, 300,000 units per week was the ceiling. I was happy with $600,000 per week, but Doc wanted more. He told me about another guy who he had met while in jail, and how he wanted to bring this guy to San Diego to broker a new deal. He said this guy had a contact in San Diego who wanted to buy 5,000 units the first week, and if they liked the product they wanted to purchase 100,000 units the next week. I told Doc that it sounded like a setup. Think about it," I said. "We never went from selling 5,000 to 100,000 units in just one week. It took over one year for us to get to that point"

"You're just being paranoid. Don't worry, I'll cut you in on the profits," Doc assured me. He went against my advice and brought the guy to Mexico anyway. He took him on a tour of the lab and brought him to his home, which was also the same community where I lived. Saturday morning Doc called me and told me he wanted to come over and talk to me. I advised him not to bring anybody else with him. He came in with this smile on his face. "What's up?" I asked.

"The guy just left about an hour ago with the 5,000 units to San Diego. He should be back in several hours with the $25,000."

"And don't forget, like I told you, they want to buy 100,000 units next week," Doc said.

"Like I told you before, it sounds like a setup to me," I insisted.

Then Doc's phone rang. It was Maria the secretary calling him because I could hear her voice. When he finished the conversation he told me he had to go.

"Where are you going?" I asked.

"The guy already has the money in San Diego, but his car broke down and he needs me to drive there and pick him up," Doc said.

"Are you freaking crazy? Don't go, that's a setup. If he has the money, then he can walk across or catch a cab," I said.

"You're just being paranoid, mothafokka," Doc chided me.

"Hey, I'm telling you that you had better not go!" I said, more forcefully now.

Doc of course didn't listen to my advice and went across the border anyway. The DEA was waiting for him on the other side in San Diego. That would be the last day that I would ever see Doc again. Just one single deal that he had tried to pull off on his own and he was gone.

Now that Doc was gone I had to decide what to do next. Should I pack up everything and get out while I can? Maybe just move down the road to the other house before they come here? Nobody, not even Doc knew about the other home that I had purchased about three miles down the road.

Justin, Rowdy and Jimmy all came by so that we could talk. Justin told me that I should get out while I still had time. But I played it off and said, "You know what, come and get me, I'm not going anywhere."

Maybe I had watched Scarface too many times. I told all of the guys to have their phones on them at all times just in case something goes down, then they all left. It was just me and the two cats hanging out there every day. Remember, Stephanie was still in Luxembourg.

CHAPTER 29

NOW OR NEVER

Several days had passed now and I was still determined to ride it out. It was about 6:00 on a Saturday morning when the phone rang. It was one of those rare instances where I actually had gone to sleep the night before. When I heard the phone ring I woke up to answer it. "Chris, this is Maria. I'm sorry, but I came by your place to talk to you about Doc, but the DEA is sitting outside your front door right now," and she hung up. I jumped out of bed and ran to the master bathroom to check the surveillance monitors. There they were, sitting in their vans right outside my front door. "To hell with this Tony Montana crap, it's time to get the hell out of here," I muttered to myself.

I tried to call Justin but I could get no answer. Then I tried Rowdy and Jimmy, but again I got no answer. Nobody was answering the phone. Now I was in full panic mode! I thought about getting on my motorcycle and riding out in front of them but I had two cats and a lot of cash to consider. I tried calling Justin and Rowdy again but I still got no answer. Then finally Jimmy answered the phone. "What's up?" he said.

"The DEA is at my front door right now! I'm going to walk out the back door in five minutes. I need you to go to the end of the complex in exactly 15 minutes.

If I make it that far I will jump the wall in exactly 15 minutes. Pick me up there," I instructed.

I checked the monitors again. They were still sitting outside in their vans. I grabbed $10,000 and put $5,000 in each pocket, gave the cats a hug and walked out the back door. I had to hope that there was nobody watching my home from the beach or there was no way I would make it to my destination. When I walked out the back door there was a security guard standing there. I spoke to him on a regular basis because I had always given him money to keep an eye on my cars that were parked out front. "Hey, Weddo, I'm sorry but there is American police outside your front door right now," he told me.

"I know," I replied.

"Be careful," he said.

"I will, thanks. You take care, my friend," I said.

I started walking to the end of the complex. When I get there I took a chair off of somebody's patio, put it up against the fence and used it to jump over. As soon as I reached the others side Jimmy pulled up and we took off on his motorcycle to my other home. When I jumped the fence I noticed that there was a ladder laying there.

CHAPTER 30

ROOFTOP SANTAS

As soon as Jimmy and I had made it to my other house I started making more phone calls to see why nobody else had answered their phones. I was finally able to get in touch with Justin's girlfriend Xochitl who told me that my brother and his friend went to play golf. Jimmy and I went to the golf course to find my brother and his friend. When we got there they told me that no one on the golf course could be notified unless it's an emergency. I told them that it was in fact a family emergency and to go and get my brother now.

When my brother and his friend finally arrived at the clubhouse, he got an ass chewing in front of a lot of people. "I told you to keep your phone ready and you're out here playing golf while the DEA is sitting at my front door!" I admonished him.

Looking back at everything that had happened at that time, I really couldn't fault my brother for going to play golf. He was the one who told me several times to get out while I still had time, but I wanted to be like Tony Montana and say "Come and get me!" And they did come, but they still didn't get me. "Get in touch with Rowdy and you guys meet us at the other house," I said. It was cold and raining at the other house. The electricity and gas was off. "This is what we're going to do." "We're going back to other place and retrieve the money and the cats." I imply.

I told Jimmy he would be the one to ride my other bike out of the garage once we're inside. We parked the bikes at the end of the complex where nobody could see them. We grabbed the ladder and we all climbed to the rooftop of the first townhome at the end of the complex. All of the townhomes were connected so it was one continuous rooftop all the way across the complex. My townhome was at the other end so we would have to cross almost every home to make our destination. We made our way across the entire complex, jumped down into my courtyard and made it inside. Once we were in I grabbed the duffle bags out of the closet upstairs and began handing them out. I started showing everyone where the cash was and we began loading as fast as we could. Money was anywhere and everywhere. I had to tear up the walls in the hallways to retrieve most of the cash. There was also the cash hidden underneath the baseboards of all the bathrooms. The last items that I grabbed was the jewelry from the safe. In two of the duffle bags we left enough space so we could place one of the cats in each bag. I gave the key to the bike (which was a brand new CBR 900RR sport bike) to Jimmy and reminded him not to take off until I texted him. What you have to remember is that we were in Mexico, not in the United States.

The rules are different for U.S. authorities in Mexico. They're not allowed to kick your door in and come inside on their own without the assistance of Mexican authorities. So I guess they decided to just sit outside and wait for me so they could catch me on their own. Anyway, we made it across the rooftop again. Once we were safely down the road we stopped to send Jimmy a message to go. We made it back to the other house safely with the money and the cats. The cats were scared but they were ok.

It didn't take very long for Jimmy to show up. "How did it go?" I asked.

"No problem, I drove right out in front of them before they could get out of their vans. I popped a wheelie right in front of them," he bragged.

"Ok, good job," I said.

I opened one of the duffle bags and handed everyone a $5,000 bundle for their efforts. We stayed there that night to rest and come up with a plan. The next day Stephanie returned from Luxembourg. I gave her money to give to her parents so they could purchase a motorhome for us. We all stayed at my brother's high-rise apartment just outside Rosarito for several days until they arrived with a newly purchased motorhome. I hid all of the money inside the motorhome and had Stephanie and her parents drive to an RV park about five miles south of Rosarito towards Ensenada.

CHAPTER 31

GRAND THEFT AUTO

The only thing that I had moved from my townhome to the other home when Doc was arrested was the last reserve of 200,000 units of Ecstasy. I needed to do something with the Ecstasy, but I wasn't really sure what to do at the time. I decided to take a chance with Carl from Houston since I wasn't dealing with Randy anymore, and let him come pick up the last of the Ecstasy. In hindsight, I should have just hidden it somewhere until a future date, but I wasn't in a good frame of mind with the DEA chasing me.

Anyway, we had some other issues to resolve as well. I had the spare keys to Doc's cars. A brand new $100,000 Porsche 928 GTS and a $75,000 Mercedes. The only problem was that they were in the same complex where I lived, and we had just made a getaway from there. To make it even more difficult was the fact that his condo was in the back of the complex. We wouldn't be able to sneak across the rooftop like before. We would have to walk down the beach and sneak in through the back somewhere. We were certain that the law would really be on the lookout for us now. It sounded really insane to go back to the same complex again, but that's exactly what we did. We waited three days before going back. We walked several miles down the beach and entered the back of the complex.

Justin and I took the Porsche and Jimmy and Rowdy took the Mercedes. We were worried because you could hear the rumble of the Porsche from a distance when we fired it up. We needed to let the vehicles run for several minutes to let them warm up. The engines were cold from sitting for so long. Once we pulled out of the garage and headed toward the front of the complex we could see ahead the same Mexican security guard who had let me walk out the back door of my condo trying to wave us down as we approached the exit. This time he wasn't being friendly. I could see him grabbing his phone from his pocket and frantically making a phone call as he was running in our direction, and we weren't planning on stopping to say hello either.

As we approached the main road we could see about ten cars all begin to hit their lights at the same time. They all had flashing red lights on their dashboards. I could tell this wasn't going to be fun. We knew all the service roads and connecting roads on both sides of the toll road from Rosarito to Ensenada. If we could hit any long stretch of road with the cars that we had it would be easy for us to get away. We didn't have to worry about helicopters following you within five or ten minutes like back in the States. We had already discussed our escape plan.

What we would have to do was lead them in the wrong direction towards Ensenada and away from my brother's apartment back in Rosarito. There was no way that we could drive straight there because it would be too easy for them to follow us. We drove south down the service road toward Puerto Nuevo. Once we made it there we darted under the toll road on a return exit to head back north toward Rosarito on the toll road. They chased us as long as they could but once we had jumped up on the toll road we were long gone.

Once we had made it to my brother's apartment complex we pulled all the way to the back of the parking area and pulled out the car covers and covered the vehicles up before going inside. Just like that we had made yet another escape from the same complex where we had before. Now we had to figure out what to do next.

CHAPTER 32

THE FEDERALES

Stephanie was still with the RV, cats, parents, and all the money in an RV park south of Rosarito just off the toll road towards Ensenada. We knew that we had to leave soon and go further into Mexico. I still had the final 200,000 units of Ecstasy that I needed to do something with. Now that Randy was out of the picture, Carl had eased his way into being the lead distributor. It really didn't matter which one of them got the merchandise. Remember, they went all the way back to high school together. They grew up together. I'm certain Randy was waiting somewhere in the wings to get something out of the last shipment. In the back of my mind I knew that I was probably giving these guys a chance to rip me off since everyone knew that it was the last of the supply, but I was out of options with the DEA looking everywhere for me. Now it was several days later after we had gone back and taken the cars. From here on I would always take my motorcycle back and forth to my brother's apartment to the RV park just in case I needed to make a fast getaway. I would always take the toll road past my old home. From the toll road I could see Mexican authorities coming out the front door with anything that they could carry out. It looked like a free for all, but it was the least of my worries now.

The next evening I told Stephanie that I needed to go back to my brother's one more time to meet Carl. I told her to stay ready because we would be heading out after that. When Carl showed up at my brother's I gave him the last of the Ecstasy. "Don't worry, I'll make sure you get your money," he promised.

"Ok, I'm trusting you," I said.

After Carl was gone, I decided to place a bet on a basketball game that night before we left town. Justin and Rowdy said they would go into Rosarito and place the bet for me. In the back of my mind I knew this might not be a good idea since we were known at the sports books for placing big bets. I told Justin that whatever you do be sure and watch your back when you leave there to make sure nobody follows you and come straight back.

It was probably about 45 minutes after they had left for the sports book when I started worrying. "It shouldn't take that long for them to place a bet and return," I said to Jimmy.

"Don't worry, they're probably having a drink, maybe you're just being paranoid," Jimmy said.

Another 45 minutes passed. Now it had been 90 minutes since they had left. At that point, I was really getting worried. They weren't answering the phone either. After almost two hours they finally returned. I went to take a look down from the 10th story balcony from my brother's apartment, and sure enough I could see a Jeep Cherokee sitting in the corner of the parking lot. It was backed in with its parking lights on. "Bro, what took you guys so long?" I asked.

"They told me when I went to the counter to place the bet that the computer was down, and it would take a while before it was working again. They told us to have free drinks and food while we waited," he said.

"I've never been there when they told me the computer was down and I couldn't place a bet," I said. "Let me ask you something. When you left there did you check your rearview mirror like I told you to make sure nobody followed you?"

When I asked my brother this question I looked him straight in the eye, and when he answered me he looked away as if to think about it. "Yeah, I checked my back," he said.

But I already had my answer because the eyes never lie. "No you didn't because there's a Jeep Cherokee backed up in the corner down there right now that followed you," I told him.

"You're just being paranoid," he said.

"Ok, guys, listen to me. The law is down there right now. I'm going down that elevator, getting on my bike and getting the hell out of here. Does anybody else want to take my advice and leave while you can?" I asked. "Ok, nobody wants to listen to me, I'm out of here," I declared.

Nobody really had anything to say. "Ok, I'm out of here," I said. I grabbed my helmet and got on the elevator to the underground parking. I put my helmet on and fired up the bike. Maybe I wasn't as crazy as Jimmy on a bike, but I always believed that I was a pretty good rider myself. If I was right about this Jeep Cherokee sitting outside then I would get to find out really quick what kind of rider I was.

The bike was warmed up now. I tightened the strap on my helmet and gathered my thoughts. It was time to go. I hit the button to raise the garage door. It only took seconds for me to realize that I was right. As soon as I shot out of there I could see the Jeep turn on his lights and begin to pull out. I knew that the only way for me to get away would be for me to get up on the toll road heading back south toward the RV park and Ensenada. But in order for me to do that I would have to travel back north down the service road towards Rosarito to enter the toll road. I had it all planned out in my mind how to get back, but what I didn't account for was all the traffic on the roads because it was the weekend. I shot up to the service road really fast. There was a lot of traffic in both directions.

It was a Friday night and there was so much traffic that I couldn't pull out. I could see in my mirrors the Jeep Cherokee approaching me rapidly. He was getting closer by the second, but I couldn't find an opening. Finally, he pulled right up next to me and began yelling something in Spanish at me. This time it wasn't the DEA. It was definitely the Federales. He must have had about ten gold chains on. There was a little revolving red flashing light on his dash. He put the Jeep in park and pulled a gun as he exited the vehicle.

I didn't even bother to check the traffic anymore. I pulled right out in front of traffic. Cars went everywhere off the road to avoid me. Now the chase was on! I couldn't hit the gas like I wanted to because of the traffic. This guy was right on my ass. I wasn't able to get any distance between us. We were both driving right down the middle, splitting traffic in both directions. If I could just get to the ramp that entered the toll road I felt like I could make it. From my brother's apartment to the ramp to enter the toll road was approximately three miles. That was the longest three miles of my life! When I finally made it to the ramp I would have to cut the bike back and do a 180 degree turn to enter the toll road.

As soon as I hit the ramp to turn back I felt my back tire being tapped by the front end of the Jeep. When he hit me from behind, the back end of the bike literally jumped several feet to the left, but I kept it in the gas and the bike quickly straightened up. I still had control of the bike as I jumped up on the toll road. As I approached the toll booths where you pay I could quickly see that I had another problem. There were no openings! I had to slow down for a moment to scan the booths again. This gave the Federales time to get right back on me. Finally, I spotted a booth that wasn't occupied. I hit the throttle and shot straight for the booth!

The Jeep was still right on me. I remember the guy sticking his face and hands out to collect the toll as I shot by. I'll never forget the look on his face. The Jeep remained on my tail as I passed through the toll booth, but with nothing in front of me now except open road the odds now were sure to change! I remember Jimmy telling me one time that if you're ever going too fast on a sport bike in a curve that you had better lay down on the tank and lean as hard as you can. It was mostly a straight shot for the first five or six miles.

I was in such a crazy mode at this time! I laid my chest as close to the tank as possible, and only occasionally glancing at my rear view mirrors. Anytime that I would see any kind of light in my rear view mirrors I would hit the throttle even more! I thought they were still right on me.

There's one serious curve after those first five or six miles of straightaway. When I hit that curve I was going so fast that I didn't think that I would make it. I leaned the bike to the left as hard as possible. Even though I was leaning the bike as hard as I could the bike was still pushing to the right. There was a barbed wire fence that separated the toll road from the service road. I was out of real estate at this point! I was so close to disaster. I was so close to hitting that barbed wire fence. I came within inches of hitting that fence.

When the bike straightened up I was quickly back on the straightaway again. Every time I saw just a glimmer of light in my mirror I would hit the throttle just a little bit more. When I finally decided to take a close look in my mirrors the Federales must have been about four or five miles behind me. When I checked my speed I was pushing 185 miles per hour! I knew they would give up on the chase with me and return to my brother's apartment.

I had to get to the RV as fast as possible and call my brother. I was going so fast that I passed the exit into the RV park! I locked up the back brakes and quickly made a U-turn back into the RV park. When I got to the RV Stephanie said, "I heard you hit the brakes on the toll road all the way from here! What's up!"

"I have to make a phone call," I said.

"Bro, get the hell out of there, I told you that you were followed. They just chased me all the way down the toll road," I said.

"Let me go downstairs and see what's up. I'll call you back," he said.

"No, bro, get the hell out of there!" I warned.

After he hung up I kept trying to call but I got no answer. Finally, after about ten minutes of calling, someone answered the phone. The person on the other end was laughing! "Ha Ha Ha. I didn't get you but I got these guys. I'll get you next," he threatened, and he hung up.

The only one who had taken my advice was Rowdy. He'd actually had enough time to get in his car and make it to the border when the Federales were chasing me down the toll road. Justin and Jimmy were taken into custody for Grand Theft Auto.

CHAPTER 33

CABO OR BUST

Rowdy called me to let me know that he made it safely across the border to San Diego. I filled him in on the bad news about Justin and Jimmy getting caught. I suggested that he rest in San Diego for a day and then join me on a journey to Cabo. Remember, my brother's girlfriend Xochitl, the girl he had met who worked at the Caliente sports book in Rosarito? One of her cousins was married to an attorney named Mario from Tijuana. I had already met with Mario a while back because for a price he promised that he could produce papers for me to stay in Mexico where nobody could touch me. I would find out from other sources after paying him that he was just feeding me a line of bullshit. If the U.S. wants you, they can come get you just about anywhere. We had paid Mario a lot of money to produce these so-called protection papers which turned out to be worthless. Before leaving for Cabo I met with Xochitl to give her money for Justin and Jimmy while they were in jail in Tijuana. I also told her to tell Mario to negotiate their release. I reminded her to tell Mario that he owed us because of the worthless protection papers he had given us. I figured that she would make him do the right thing since my brother was her boyfriend. I had to hope he could get them out.

When Rowdy got to the RV park we loaded the bike on a trailer behind the RV, and we were ready to go. I had just purchased a brand new Toyota Land Cruiser from a dealership in Tijuana. I wanted to take a vehicle with Mexican plates with us to drive down to Cabo. Rowdy drove the Land Cruiser while I drove the RV. We got on the toll road and headed south toward Ensenada. When we reached the toll booth at the end of the toll road to enter Ensenada, I noticed that they had a military checkpoint set up there. We were a little bit nervous as we passed through the checkpoint, but the military only glanced inside and looked around before letting us pass.

If you plan on traveling further into Mexico past Ensenada, you have to purchase a tourist permit. Since we were obviously traveling further than Ensenada we had to stop at a travel agency. I used my fake ID to obtain my travel permit with no problems. When we finally exited Ensenada I could tell right away that it was not going to be an easy journey. This was the first time that I had ever driven an RV. The highway was nothing more than a small winding road that curved around the edges of hillsides and mountains. Everything was right on the edge of the cliffs. As we drove you could see vehicles down in the valleys that had driven off the edge at some point in time!

When big trucks would pass us going in the other direction they would take up so much of the narrow road that I was certain we would either be hit or pushed off the edge, and there were very few guardrails! When we finally made it through the winding roads on the edge of the cliffs the roads straightened out but they were still very narrow.

I'm not sure how many hours we drove before making it to a place called Guerrero Negro. This is the city where you must pass through another military checkpoint before driving even further into Mexico. As we pulled up to the checkpoint we had to try and not show that we were nervous in any way, but it's hard to do when you have military guys with guns enter the RV and begin looking around ... especially when you have over 1.5 million in cash stashed! They opened the cabinets, then looked under the cushions on the couch, and checked the bathroom area before heading to the room in the back. All of the cash was stashed under the bed and behind the TV cabinets in the back. That sure was a truly nerve wracking point for us. They ended up only looking inside the drawers before returning to the front of the RV. They checked out our travel permits and motioned for us to go ahead.

We continued driving for several more hours before finally making it to Cabo. We found an RV park to stay at right next to the beach.

CHAPTER 34

THE COMANDANTE

For the next several weeks we hung out at the beach and relaxed during the day. At nighttime we would go out to eat at different restaurants around town and see what Cabo had to offer. Anything that we could do to ease our minds about everything that had gone wrong back in Rosarito.

Now I had something new to worry about. Stephanie was pregnant with our first child. After several more weeks in Cabo, I began to get bored, and decided to go and place a bet on a basketball game for that night. They also have the Caliente sports book in Cabo just like back in Rosarito and Tijuana. You would think that I would have learned my lesson from the problems in Rosarito, but I guess I was a little hard headed to say the least. Obviously they were looking for us through the sports books there, so it wouldn't be that hard to put the word out to every sports book on the coast, but that didn't stop me. I told Stephanie and Rowdy to go into town with me to Caliente to bet on a game. We went to the sports book where I placed my bet quickly. I didn't want to stay long after what had happened to Justin and Jimmy back in Rosarito. We were only there about 20 minutes before leaving. I decided not to cash in my winning basketball ticket from when I sent my brother just in case they were tracking that ticket.

When we got to the vehicle to leave we were immediately surrounded by police. "Follow us to the police station," the officer said.

"They probably were waiting for us to show up at any of the sports books," Stephanie said.

"You guys just stay calm and let's see what's up," I told them.

When we got there it was a very small building that said Policia on the front. It didn't look like much of a police station, but remember this is Mexico. They told Stephanie and Rowdy to stay in the vehicle and they escorted me inside. When I got inside there was a big Mexican guy sitting behind his desk staring at me. "Have a seat, gringo," he said. "Do you know why I brought you in?" he asked.

"No I don't, sir," I replied.

"I brought you in because you're driving a brand new Toyota Land Cruiser with Mexico plates and we don't sell that vehicle here in Mexico yet," he said. "Where did you buy that vehicle?" he asked.

"I bought it in Tijuana," I replied.

"Do you have the number for the dealership in Tijuana?" he asked.

I gave him the telephone number from a card in my wallet and he began making a call. "You don't mind if I call and check do you?" he asked.

"No, not at all," I replied. What else could I say?

"Hello, this is the Comandante from the Police in Cabo. I have a gringo here who says he purchased a Toyota Land Cruiser at your dealership."

"I don't believe that this model is sold in Mexico," he said.

"Yes, this is a new model in Mexico now, and the gringo did purchase the vehicle from us," the person on the other end of the phone told him.

"Ok, thank you very much," and the Comandante hung up the phone. "Ok, so you did buy the vehicle legally in Mexico," he said. The Comandante leaned back in his chair and started taking a closer look at my Mexican driver's license. In Mexico, all that I needed was money to pay someone to get me a real Mexican driver's license. The only problem was that I spoke very little Spanish and I started to worry that the Comandante might begin questioning me on how I have a Mexican driver's license but speak very little Spanish. I knew he was looking for another angle to hem me up. "What kind of work do you do?" he asked.

I knew that I needed to do something to get out of this situation. It probably wouldn't take him very many more phone calls to figure out who I was. "I'm a professional gambler," I replied. At that point, I pulled out the winning ticket that I still had in my wallet from when Justin and Rowdy had placed the bet for me back in Rosarito. It was a $2,000 ticket from a basketball game, and since it was a winning ticket it was worth almost $4,000.

"I want you to have this ticket," I said. He took the ticket and began looking at with a puzzled look on his face. "That ticket is worth almost $4,000 dollars," I told him.

"So, if I go to the sports book and give them this ticket then they're going to give me almost $4,000?" he said.

"Yes, sir," I replied.

"And why would you want to do that for me?" he asked.

"This is what I do for a living and I'm very good at what I do, so I want to give you a gift and if I ever need you for anything you can return the favor someday," I explained.

"Ok, so if I have any problem with the ticket where can I find you?" he asked.

"I'm staying at the RV park right next to the beach. If you have any problem you can find me there," I told him. I didn't want to lie to him just in case they followed us.

"Ok, you have a nice vacation here in Cabo. You're free to go," he said.

"Thank you, Comandante," I said as I was leaving his office. And just like that I walked right out the front door of the Police station.

As soon as I got back in the vehicle Stephanie and Rowdy both began questioning me about what had happened. "What's going on?" they asked.

"Don't worry about it, everything is ok, I just gave the Comandante my winning ticket from Caliente, and he was happy with that," I said.

CHAPTER 35

NOWHERE TO RUN

W e spent the next four or five days figuring out our next option. We had already traveled as far south as possible to Cabo. When I was on the run back home I always traveled back and forth in the direction of trouble and it somehow had worked out for me. We only had one option here. We would have to drive back towards Ensenada and Rosarito. It sounded crazy, but we really had no other option. It was probably just a matter of time before the Comandante would come here looking for us.

It was almost a week now since I had left the Comandante's office. I told Stephanie and Rowdy to pack up and prepare to drive back in the same direction from which we came. I could only hope that the same strategy of going back into the eye of the storm would work for us just like it did for me back in the States. Sounds really crazy, but that's what the plan was.

The next morning we left Cabo and headed back north. The plan was to try to make it back to Ensenada and find a home there. Ensenada was about an hour's drive from the border. Rosarito was only about 20 minutes from the border. Going back to Rosarito was not an option for us, so Ensenada would hopefully be the next best thing but we had a long way back to get there.

The biggest concern for me was the military checkpoint that we would have to go back through again in Guerrero Negro about two hours out of Cabo. What if the authorities had notified every military and police station all the way down the coast from Rosarito to Cabo? What if the Comandante had notified the checkpoint to be on the lookout for a gringo in an RV? All of these questions started going through my mind. It was that same "gut feeling" that had been right so many times for me. I was getting tired of this "gut feeling" all the time. I remember back in Texas when I had plenty of time to think about that Huntsville State Prison sign. Now I had two hours to drive and think about that military checkpoint in Guerrero Negro.

We were getting closer to the checkpoint when I decided to pull over and remind Rowdy to not be nervous in any way as he was following us with the Land Cruiser. We had already been through so many close calls together that they had also perfected the art of looking calm, cool, and collected. As we entered the checkpoint I could see up ahead the soldiers with their guns by their side. We pulled up and the soldiers motioned for us to stop. They didn't look very friendly either. When I stopped and opened the door, this time they didn't rush onto the RV like they did before when we were going the other direction.

In fact, this time they didn't enter the RV at all. Instead, one of the soldiers pointed at me and said, "You, come with me." I got off of the RV and followed him into the office. This didn't feel like a good situation. "Have a seat there, gringo," he said.

I took a seat and watched the soldier go over to a wall phone and make a call. I tried not to show that I was nervous. *Would this finally be the end of the road?* I thought to myself. If he was calling us in we were sitting ducks here. He was talking in Spanish on the phone while staring at me at the same time. After several minutes on the phone he motioned for me to come to the phone and he handed it to me. "Hello," I said.

"Gringo, this is the Comandante back in Cabo. I notified my men to be on the lookout for you. I had come by the RV park where you were staying to thank you for the money, but you were already gone. If you're ever in Cabo again and you need anything, you let me know. I've instructed my men to let you pass through," he said.

"Thank you, Comandante. When I come back to Cabo again I'll be sure to come see you," I told him.

I handed the phone back to the soldier. "You're free to go," he said.

"Ok, thank you," I replied as I walked out the door.

CHAPTER 36

MR. MAGOO

Now that we had somehow made it thru the checkpoint and were several miles down the road, Stephanie and Rowdy both began questioning me about what had just happened. "You're not going to believe this. The soldier told me to have a seat while he made a phone call. When he handed me the phone it was the Comandante back in Cabo. He thanked me for the money and told me he had ordered the military to let me pass through," I said.

We continued driving towards Ensenada. We were hopeful that we could find some place to stay there. We drove through the night, and the next day we finally made it to Ensenada. I remembered one time Stephanie and I had taken a drive to a tourist spot in Ensenada called "La Bufadora". It's one of the few "Blowholes" in the world where the ocean water shoots straight up in the air as it hits the oceanside. I remember seeing some very nice homes that were right on the beach on our way there. We decided to head in that direction to see what we could find. When we arrived at the front gate of the community (called Baja Beach), there was a security guard waiting to greet us. I asked him who we could talk to about either renting or buying a home in the community. He gave us directions to the home of someone named Ed Phinney.

When we pulled up to the home we could see him and his wife sitting on the front porch in their rocking chairs. We walked to the front porch to talk to him. He was an old, short guy wearing a big straw hat. "He resembles Mr. Magoo," I whispered to Stephanie. "Hi, good afternoon, sir, how are you?" I greeted.

"I'm fine thank you, I'm Ed Phinney and this is my wife," he said as he leaned back in his chair and sipped on his lemonade. He gave us that look as if to say, "I'm being nice, but you guys are interrupting my lemonade on the porch with my wife."

He then asked, "So, what brings you to the neighborhood?"

"Do you have any homes for rent or for sale?" I asked.

He leaned back in his chair again, sipped on his lemonade, and replied, "No, we don't have anything around here for rent, but we have homes here for sale if you happen to have $170,000."

"I have cash, will that work for you?" I said.

"Oh yeah, yeah; honey, get me the keys and let's show these nice people around," he said as he almost fell out of his chair and spilled his lemonade. He and his wife took us on a tour of three brand new homes. "Take your pick, they're all brand new and they're all the same price of $170,00," he said.

"Give me just a few minutes with my wife please," I responded.

After returning from my conversation with Stephanie, I said to him, "Ok, we'll take this home. Can we move in tonight?" I asked.

"Let me call the owner," he replied. "Did you say you're paying cash?" he asked.

"Yes, I'll pay cash," I said.

He got on his phone and made a call. "The owner says you can pay me the cash and I'll give you a receipt. The owner will be down tomorrow, but you can go ahead and move in today," he told me.

"Give me a few minutes," I said.

I went out to the RV and counted out $170,000 in $100's and returned to the house. "Here you are, Mr. Phinney, $170,000. Would you like to count it out?" I asked.

"No, it's ok, I trust you. I will count it later. Go ahead and move in and make yourself at home," he said.

We finally had a place to call home for now. We moved our belongings and the money into the home and called it a day. It had been a crazy and long journey to get here. Rowdy wanted to go back to the States. I told him that I wasn't sure if that was a good idea, but he wanted to go anyway. I thanked him for all of his help and he was off. I told him that I was still doing everything to get my brother and Jimmy out of prison in Tijuana, and to be careful and stay in touch.

Stephanie was starting to show and was only several months away from giving birth. News started coming back about everything going on back in the States, and it wasn't good at all. Doc had rolled on everyone in the organization including myself to save his own ass. He accepted a plea deal for ten years. He put everything on me, including telling the authorities that I was the owner of the lab in Mexico, even though the business was in his name. You know how it works. If you're the first one to rat then everyone else gets the blame, and the most time. I wasn't a killer or murderer, but I was still a wanted drug dealer who couldn't be caught. The longer that I could elude authorities, the more they wanted me. Was I proud of what I had become? No, but it is what it is.

I had to keep moving on. We settled into our new home at Baja Beach in Ensenada. I purchased two brand new four-wheelers so Stephanie and I could take rides down the beach in the afternoons. A few months later our first child Brandon was born. I started taking him for rides on the four-wheeler in a backpack seat. When he was old enough to ride on the front I would let him drive and give it the gas on his own. I did everything possible to take my mind off of everything going on back in the States.

My attorney informed me that not only was everyone going down, but there were plenty of people already pointing the finger at me. Doc had snitched on everyone in the organization, including myself. Slowly but surely everyone began to fall like dominoes. The longer that I eluded prosecution the worse it got for me. I was wanted for purchasing and manufacturing a controlled substance back in Dallas. I also had a fugitive charge. Now, according to my attorney I had a new International manufacturing and distribution charge on top of everything else. But no matter what, I tried to stay positive and keep going no matter how hopeless it seemed sometimes. What else could I do? There were no other options now. That meant keep going and keep doing everything possible to stay free.

I started meeting some new friends in the neighborhood. There was Eddy right down the street who worked on cars and then there was Ron the contractor who lived a few blocks over from me. Justin and Jimmy were still locked up. We continued to wait for some kind of good news about them. I continued to send more and more money to the lawyer to hopefully win their release. Justin's girlfriend Xochitl informed me that they were getting closer to gaining their freedom.

CHAPTER 37

THE GOOD, THE BAD
AND THE UGLY

finally got the call from Xochitl that they would be releasing my brother and Jimmy in several days. There was only one problem that confronted them. When you're a U.S. citizen in in prison across the border, you're supposed to be released to U.S. authorities back into your own country. If they were released to U.S. authorities there was a good chance that they might be picked up by the Feds and go straight to jail in the States. The attorney in Mexico had informed Xochitl that he was making sure that they would be released on Mexican soil. Two days later Xochitl called to inform me that Justin and Jimmy were being released at 10:00 that morning. At 11:00, Justin and Jimmy arrived in downtown Ensenada to meet Rowdy and I.

After we made certain that nobody was following us we all headed to my home for a celebration. It was like old times again having everyone together. It was a moment when we could all temporarily forget about all the problems back home. Rowdy had been going back and forth to the States and nobody had picked him up yet. I reminded everyone that if you stay in the U.S. sooner or later they will come for you. But all of them had lives back in the U.S. and they all wanted to go back. The next day they all left for San Diego.

All of the guys would come down to see me on occasion. I always reminded them about what could happen if they didn't watch their backs. They always assured me that nobody had followed them to my house. I'm sure that spending over one year in jail in Tijuana is more than enough to remind someone not to make the same mistake twice.

Deep down I knew that there was big trouble back home. We did whatever we could to take our minds off of everything. At that point we still had money, Brandon was one year old now and Stephanie was pregnant with our second child. But several months later my worst fears for the guys came to fruition. I got word that the authorities had taken Rowdy and Jimmy into custody. The following week they arrested Justin at his job in San Diego. Now it was official, I was "The Last of the Mohicans". Everyone was now behind bars except me. It was obvious now that I would never see any money from the last of the Ecstasy that I had given Carl. It took several months of constantly calling before I was finally able to get in touch with him. I could tell by the tone of his voice that he wasn't going to hold up his end of the deal. After I told him that I needed my money he immediately went into "defense mode" by saying, "So you're threatening me if I don't pay you?"

At that point I just hung up. For all I knew he could have been recording the conversation. It's funny how money always brings out the true person in everyone. That's what I get for dealing with a slimy snake like Carl. In the drug business there are always plenty of shady characters. If Carl would have ripped off the Mexican drug cartel we all know what would have happened to him. My philosophy was always just to write it off as a cost of doing business and move on. I had multiple offers from people asking if I wanted them to go and collect my money from Carl. My response was always, "No, let it go." I never went after anyone who ripped me off. I was always a true believer that what goes around comes around. Maybe in other countries there is honor, but in the U.S. everybody is out for themselves. They either rip you off or rat on you, or both.

Several months later in November of '97, sentences started coming down. Justin was sentenced to four years for money laundering. Rowdy was sentenced to 2.5 years for money laundering. Randy was sentenced to 7.5 years for conspiracy to commit money laundering. Brett in Houston was sentenced to three years for money laundering. and Carl was charged with conspiracy to commit money laundering and structuring transactions to evade reporting requirements. He was sentenced to eight years in Federal prison. He had recently finished his law degree at Texas A&M.

He was also disbarred from ever practicing law. I told you what goes around comes around. I wasn't sure what Jimmy's status was at that point or how much time he had been given, but what I did know was that everybody within the organization was locked up except me. I couldn't stop to think of how many times and how many years now that I had escaped justice. All that I could do now was continue to try and stay free since Stephanie had another baby on the way.

CHAPTER 38

RETURN OF THE FEDERALES

I always wanted one of those frozen margarita machines like you see behind the bars. Or like the big Slurpee machines that you see at 7-11. The best ones are made by Hobart, and they're not cheap either. The one that I wanted was $10,000 if purchased brand new. I was able to find one out of Los Angeles that was six months old for $5,000. It cost me another $500 to have it delivered to our home in Ensenada. I would still have to buy a stand for it, but for the meantime it sat on the porcelain tile floor in the entry hall. After it sat there for several days I decided to try it out. I told Stephanie that Brandon and I were taking a ride to the local liquor store. I decided to make frozen pina coladas the first time, so I purchased Rum 151, pineapple juice, and coconut juice for this first round. After putting all the ingredients in, I turned it on and let it run. Just like that I had a frozen drink machine running in my home! Albeit it was still sitting in the front entry hall of my home.

Brandon was still with me while I was doing all of this. I had to go to the restroom so I left him there temporarily. I was only gone for several minutes but I returned only to see Brandon sitting in a pool of pina colada with 151 proof rum!

He was licking his fingers. I picked him up and yelled for his mom to come and get him. As she took him I got a royal ass chewing. "You need to watch him every second . It could kill him if he gets too much alcohol in his system" she says. "Hey, he has to start sometime ," I say jokingly. She didn't think it was so funny. I knew that she was right but I didn't want to admit it. I began cleaning up the mess when I hear a knock at the front door." Who can this be

?" I thought to myself. When I open the front door it's not what I want to see! It's a group of Federales standing there. Please come with us ," one of the Federales says. By this time Stephanie was half-way down the stairs to see who it was. "It's the Federales," I say with a worried look on my face. I have to go with them," I say. I could tell that the worried look on her face wasn't about Brandon anymore. As I walk outside my home I can see my 2 local friends Ron and Eddie and a host of Federal Police cars in the road. My first thought was that they had suspected something about me and called the police. "Is that your truck? The Federale asks. "Si", I reply. "Follow us please," he says. I get in my truck, and start it up. I'm thinking to myself "this can't be good."

I began following Eddie and Ron in their vehicles behind a line of Federal Police cars. I was wondering if this was the end of the road for me? "Were we on our way to the police station for interrogation? To my surprise we didn't make a turn toward the front gate, but instead we turned right, directly toward the beach. We ended up pulling over right behind the Federales and they began directing us to follow them as they walked to the beach. What could this be about? I continually asked myself as we moved closer and closer to the beach. I could see some large, strange-looking bundles that were wrapped up and taped. They lined the beach as far as you could see. I walked closer to Ron and Eddie, and asked, "What's going on?"

"There was a drug running ship that sank last night," Ron said.

"Those are bundles of marijuana that floated to the shore. They don't have enough vehicles to transfer the bundles to the police station, and they asked us to help them," Ron said.

Obviously I was still nervous. Here I am a wanted fugitive drug trafficker helping the Federales load bundles of marijuana into the back of my truck!

Once all of the vehicles were loaded the caravan was off and moving. I had one Federale in the front seat with me and two more in the back seat of my truck. There were also two more riding in the back with the marijuana. I had to do my best to pretend as though I wasn't nervous. The Federale riding in the front with me asked, "What's your name, quero?"

"David Bush," I replied.

"And what kind of work do you have in Mexico?" he asked.

"I'm a professional gambler," I replied.

Lucky for me, it didn't take long for us to reach the police station because I didn't want to answer any more questions.

As soon as we arrived everyone began unloading the bundles from the back of my truck. "Muchas gracias for your help," one of the Federales said as he shook my hand.

When I returned to the house Stephanie asked me what happened? "You're not going to believe me," I told her. "They needed us to use our vehicles to help them transport bundles of marijuana that floated up onto the beach."

She couldn't believe it either.

After everything that had happened, I still never got the opportunity to try out my new daiquiri machine. Between Brandon pulling the lever on my first attempted batch and then the Federales showing up at my door, I needed a drink! I went back to the liquor store and purchased all of the supplies once more. Only this time I put two bottles of Rum 151 in the mix instead of one. After several hours of running I decided to try it. It was so good of a machine that I could barely taste the alcohol, or maybe I was just used to having strong drinks. I decided to give Eddie a call and have him come over and try one for himself. I hooked him up with a big glass and he started drinking it fast. "Hey, you should take it easy because there's a lot of alcohol in there," I said.

"This is pretty good, but I can barely taste the alcohol," Eddie said.

"Trust me, it has plenty of alcohol," I assured him.

Eddie was a big guy. He downed the first glass fast and asked, "Is it okay if I take another glass with me?"

"Are you sure? There's a lot of alcohol in there," I replied.

"Yeah, I'm fine, I just live right down the road," Eddie told me.

I made him another big glass. He thanked me and off he went. About ten minutes later my phone rang. "Hey, this is Eddie, I didn't make it home. I ran off the road and into the ditch. Can you come and help me?" he said.

"I'm on my way," I replied.

When I arrived, Eddie was standing on the side of the road still drinking his Pina Colada. He was laughing even though his truck was down in the ditch. "It sort of sneaked up on me," he explained.

"Are you okay?" I asked.

"Yeah, I'm okay," he said, "but do you think we can get another one of those Pina Colada's?"

"I don't think you need another one right now. Let's get your truck out of the ditch and get you home before the police get here," I told him. I grabbed a rope behind my seat, and somehow even though Eddie could barely walk, we were able to pull the truck out of the ditch. Then I followed him the other half mile down the road to ensure that he made it home.

CHAPTER 39

THE ROOT OF ALL EVIL

After Stephanie had our second child (Hailey) she started becoming ill, sometimes to the point where she would feel like passing out. We weren't certain what the problem was. One day she began looking yellow and pale and I drove her to the Military Hospital. That was the only place close to where we lived on the outskirts of Ensenada, but they couldn't determine what the problem was. The next day she was taking the kids for a walk in their stroller when she fainted. Luckily for us it happened right in front of Ed Phinney's house. (The old man who had sold me the house). Ed Phinney rushed to my house to tell me to come quickly! We put her into Ed's van and left the kids with his wife. "There's a really good doctor named Dr. Shinohara in Ensenada. We have to take her there," Ed said.

When we arrived at the doctor's office we got her inside. Ed and I waited in the lobby while the doctor examined her. Finally the doctor came out into the lobby and asked me to follow him into his office. "Please have a seat," the doctor said. "Your wife has kidney stones that are blocking her system," he told me. "We don't have the kind of medical facility to handle this problem here in Ensenada. She needs immediate attention back in the U.S. or she could die," the doctor said grimly.

Now I was at another crossroad once again. This would force me to tell the doctor of our situation. "Doctor, we have a problem. We have two children that need their mother. If we put her on a plane back to the U.S. then there's a good chance she will be arrested for money laundering as soon as she steps foot on U.S. soil, but if it means saving her life then we have no choice but to send her. If there's any way of treating her here, then money is not an issue," I told him.

"Let me make some phone calls," the doctor replied. After the doctor made about four or five phone calls, he said, "We can perform the surgery here, but it won't be cheap because we have to fly in several surgeons along with myself, a nutritionist and a nurse. Also, I must remind you that this is a very serious situation. Your wife is very ill, and there is no guarantee that she will make it through surgery even if she was in the U.S, but I can assure that these are some of the best surgeons we have in Mexico."

"Okay, then let's do it," I replied.

When the meeting was over I returned to the lobby to inform Ed Phinney that she will be having the operation here. I left Stephanie at the doctor's office, and they would soon be moving her to the local hospital, while I returned with Ed to his home to pick up the kids.

In the meantime, Stephanie was feeling well enough to contact her mother Connie back in Oklahoma to let her know that she was very sick and in the hospital. The next day her mom flew to San Diego and I picked her up in Tijuana. Before Stephanie had become ill we had fought a lot about her family. Her dad was a used car salesman in Oklahoma. When he had wanted to start his own used car lot I loaned him $70,000 to get started, but after several months of being in business he decided to sell off the inventory, and use to the money to pay off his home, and return to his old job. I also had a problem with her brother Allen who lived in Houston. Several months back, I needed someone to pick up $250,000 from a friend of mine who owned a Cabaret in Houston. I told her brother Allen to take $50,000 off the top just for driving across town to pick up the money for me, and to keep the remaining $200,000 for me until Stephanie's parents could bring the money to us when they came to visit us in Mexico. The only problem was, when they arrived to our home in Ensenada several months later, they only showed up with $125,000! To say that I was irate was an understatement! When I asked Stephanie to call her brother to find out where the rest of my money was, the message I got? "Tell Chris that I'm sorry, I got a little carried away.

I bought myself a new motorhome, and my wife a new Lexus," he told her.

Stephanie had always told me that I could always trust her family with money. I was finding out that definitely wasn't the case. I was certain that Stephanie had told her mom about my displeasure with her family. I could tell by the looks that I would get from her mom that there was no longer a love affair between her family and I. The only concern at the time, however, was Stephanie making it through the operation. Sometimes those snarly looks that her mom would give me while she was outside the house puffing on her cigarette made me want to blow up and ask her where my money was. In reality, I knew that money was gone, and I would never see it again. It's funny how when you give people money, they think you're the greatest, but when you ask for it back, you're the worst guy in the world.

Before Stephanie went into surgery, the doctor came into the lobby to tell her mom and I that this type of surgery usually takes about an hour. If it was sooner than that, then usually the operation was not successful. I remember when the doctor returned to the lobby, I was really nervous because he returned about an hour and 15 minutes later. "Everything went well," the doctor told us. But even with the good news, I could still see a snarly look coming from her mother.

We brought Stephanie home and she began her recovery. That was a good thing, but the bad thing was that her mom was still staying with us to help with the kids. I was hoping that she would go back to Oklahoma sooner than later.

Several days later I told Stephanie that I was taking Brandon with me to the store. With Brandon in my arms I passed my mother-in-law as I was walking down the stairs. She grabbed Brandon from me and said, "You're not going anywhere with him."

I grabbed Brandon back and told her, "You're not going to come into my house and tell me that I'm not going anywhere with my own son. You're damn lucky that Stephanie made it through the operation, because if she hadn't then I would have taken my kids and gone deep into Mexico, and you would never see them again."

Stephanie got out of bed, came to the top of the stairs and said, "It's okay, Mom, let them go, they'll be back."

CHAPTER 40

THE FINAL ENCOUNTER

It was a big relief for me to see Stephanie's mom finally leave, but things were never really the same again between Stephanie and I. I often used meth as a way to try and forget about all of the problems that I had. Sometimes we would argue about the money, and I would fly into a rage and begin destroying something in the house. I remember one day where I kicked all of the cabinets out of the master bedroom closet and threw everything over the upstairs patio into the driveway downstairs. I could never get over the fact that her family had so blatantly ripped me off. If she could have admitted that her family was wrong then I could have let it go, but instead she defended them, and angered me more by saying that they did nothing wrong. You know the old saying "Blood is thicker than Water."

After several more months had passed, Stephanie informed me that her mom was coming back again to visit the kids. I wasn't very happy to hear that. It was in the back of my mind that she could be bringing the law back with her to get me, but I dismissed that notion for whatever reason. When her mom arrived at our home with Stephanie I could tell that she still held her vindictive attitude toward me. She ended up staying for several weeks.

One night Stephanie asked me if I could drive her to Tijuana to drop her Mom off at the border. "Then we can take the kids and go out to eat and go to the mall," she said. I thought it would be a good idea to take the kids out, and I was ready to get rid of her mom. *Maybe this was a chance to work on our relationship?* I thought to myself.

The next morning we put the kids into their car seats and began our drive to Tijuana. Stephanie rode in the back with the kids, and her mom rode in the front. It was about a 40-minute drive from where we lived in Ensenada to the border in Tijuana. There's an area at the border called Centro where the taxis drop off and pick up people. When we arrived I pulled up to the curb and put the truck in park. At this point I reached to the back seat to take Brandon and hold him, but out of the corner of my eye, I could see men with guns running as fast as possible to surround my truck! As I turned around to take a closer look I could tell that they were both American and Mexican federal agents. They all had guns pointed directly at me! As I tried to get out of the truck, my mother-in-law grabbed Brandon from me, and she had that snarly look on her face as though she had just got the last laugh!

This time I knew that I was in big trouble! There were so many guns pointed at me from every direction that I knew there was no chance for escape this time! They immediately took Stephanie and I into custody. I tried to give one of the agents my fake ID, but he told me, "Don't worry, Chris, we already know about your six or seven fake names."

I knew this was the end of the road for me. They put us in an unmarked car, and just like that we were being driven away! I could see my mother-in-law getting into the driver's seat of my truck and preparing to drive away with my two kids. As we were being driven away, I remember thinking to myself of all the times that I had escaped justice for so many years, but only to finally be done in by my mother-in-law. I often wondered when everything would come to an end. It was a constant grind on the mind to stay free over the years. It had taken them over two years after Doc's capture to finally catch me. I had been on the run for almost ten years. From the time I was 24 , to the time I was 34. June 6th, 1998 would be the day it would all come to an end. Finally done in by the in-laws.

CHAPTER 40

CHAPTER 41

THE CAMERAS

Once we had arrived at the police headquarters in Tijuana, they held us in a cell together. We weren't sure what was going on in the next room, but we could hear a lot of people talking and moving around. Several minutes later one of the Federales came in and said to us, "The U.S. Marshals want to take you both back to San Diego right now. But we have to follow due process in Mexico. That means that you both will be flown to Mexico City and placed in a jail until extradition is determined."

A few minutes later some more Federales entered the holding cell and began escorting us to a large room full of people and cameras everywhere. We were completely surrounded by reporters with their microphones in hand, and bright lights all around. I recognized the logos of about every local news channel. They stuck the microphones in front of us, and began asking us questions. "How long have you been in Mexico?" "What was your purpose here?" "Where are you from?" The questions were coming from all directions. Stephanie whispered to me, "Don't say anything." After the reporters realized that we weren't going to answer any questions, they turned off the lights and cameras. Afterward they placed us into a Federal police car and began escorting us to the airport. There was a convoy of Federal Police cars in front of us and behind us.

When we arrived at the airport, there was a PGR Federal Lear Jet waiting for us. Once again, there were reporters and cameras everywhere. They escorted us onto the plane and seated us. They fastened our seatbelts for us since we were handcuffed. There were two Federal agents seated facing us, and two behind us. As the jet started and the agents began closing the door, I could see from the window the reporters with their flashing cameras, still taking pictures of the jet even as we were moving toward the runway. Several minutes later we were airborne, on our way to someplace called Mexico City. Somewhere that we had never been before.

When we arrived at the airport in Mexico City, there were more reporters and cameras to greet us as we were being escorted off of the plane. There was a convoy of Federal Police cars waiting to escort us to some Mexican prison. You would have thought they had caught Pablo Escobar or El Chapo with all of the attention we were getting! As we were being driven through the streets of Mexico City, I remember never seeing so many people in my life. The streets seemed endless, and crowded with people as far as you could see in any direction. When we finally arrived to our final destination, they informed us that Stephanie would be going to the women's side of the prison, and that I would be going to the men's side.

CHAPTER 42

THE OTHER WORLD

"If you don't have money you can sleep on the floor with the monsters," he said.

"The monsters?" I replied.

"Yes, the monsters," Oscar said. "Here in this world there are only two types, those who have money, we call them the Padrinos, and those who don't are the monsters." Then he added, "Or, if you think that you might be here for a long time, then you can purchase your own cell for a one-time fee of 5,000 dollars,"

"I'm not sure how long I will be here," I said.

"Do you have an attorney? If you don't have an attorney, then I have a good attorney," said Oscar.

"No, I don't," I replied.

"I'll call him tomorrow and ask him to come and visit us," Oscar said.

I paid Oscar the 100 dollars for my own bunk. That night, when the lights were turned off, I laid in my bunk remembering everything, and wondering what would happen to me now. All sorts of questions were running through my mind. How long would I be in this prison? What would happen to me if I return to the U.S.? Would I ever see freedom again? I kept hearing strange noises as if something was moving all around me. I got up from my bunk and turned on the light. There were cockroaches coming out of all the walls!

"What's up, Guero? You've never seen cockroaches before? Welcome to our world," Oscar said, laughing.

"I'm not use to living with cockroaches," I said.

"They just come out to get something to eat while we're sleeping," Oscar explained laughingly.

The next morning Oscar woke me up. "Come on, guero, we have to move outside."

There was a revision going on. The guards, or Custodios as they call them, ordered everyone outside in lines facing forward. Inmates from all the dormitories were all forming lines so that we could all be accounted for, while other Custodios were going through every cell looking for contraband. There were inmates lined up in all directions as far you could imagine. "How many inmates are here?" I asked.

"Probably around 8,000, but don't talk right now. Just stand up straight and look forward," Oscar replied.

Once everyone was accounted for, we all began our return to the dormitories. When we returned to our cell, Oscar said, "There's probably only four or five Americans in this entire prison. When you go anywhere in this prison, don't go by yourself, or you will get jumped and robbed."

I noticed that everyone was grabbing their towel and clothes and heading to the showers. "Why is everyone rushing to the showers?" I asked.

"Today is visitation day. You can go with us," Oscar said.

"I'll need some more clothes," I said.

"Come with me and I'll show you where they sell clothes," Oscar replies.

"They sell clothes here in prison?" I asked, surprised.

Everyone began laughing.

"Why is everyone laughing?" I said.

"They sell anything that you want here. As long as you have money there's nothing you can't have here. Money is the King here," said Oscar.

We went to the other side of the dormitory to see what kind of clothes they had. There was never a dull moment when I went somewhere. There was always someone yelling something at me in Spanish. There were rows and rows of cells with something for sale. Brand new clothes, cell phones, TV's, stereos, DVD players, watches, gold chains, or anything you wanted. "You can have any-thing that you want in here that you have outside, and even more, but the only thing that you don't have is the freedom to go outside that wall," Oscar explained.

This prison is crazy, I thought to myself.

After returning to our cell I showered, put my new clothes on, and headed to the visitation area with my cellmates. The visitation area was the same open area in the middle of the prison where we had gone for the head count during the revision in the morning. At the visitation area there were groups of people everywhere. There were tents set up across the perimeter wall. "What are the tents for?" I asked.

"The tents are for rent in case you have a girl with you and you want to go and do your thing," Oscar said.

"How many inmates have visits?" I asked. "There's a lot of people here."

"Probably about 25% of the inmates have a visit on any given day," said Oscar.

Can you picture over 2,000 inmates having a visit on any given day? Plus, the number of people that were visiting. That's a lot of people in one place at one time.

"I meet new people all the time at visitation," Oscar said.

"What are the visitation days?" I asked.

"Visitations are on Tuesday, Thursday, Friday, and Saturday, and overnight visits are on Wednesday," Oscar told me. "A lot of inmates like it here because they can spend four or five days a week with their wife, and then they get a break from her when they go home, then he can go back to his dorm and play cards with his buddies, and not have to worry about his wife nagging him 24 hours a day."

When we made it back to our dorm, the first thing that Victor said to me was, "The first thing that you need to do is learn Spanish, and we're going to teach you." "The first words that we're going to teach you are all of the bad words." The Spanish that they speak on the streets in Mexico is called chilangro, so several months later the other inmates called me Guero Chilangro. Anyway, I began to learn a new life behind bars. My attorney in the U.S. informed me that the news didn't look good for me regarding my return.

I hired Oscar's attorney in Mexico to help me with my extradition process. Remember, if you're in another country, and an attorney tells you that he can get you out of prison, and you're an American citizen, he's lying to you. The U.S. has a treaty agreement with many countries including Mexico, which means that you're going to be extradited one way or another. The only thing that you can do is appeal your extradition for a while, which is what I needed to do for now with the hope of a better deal in the U.S. In Mexico, you're allowed up to three appeals which usually take up to three years before your final appeal decision. I knew that my time here would be short-lived. In the meantime, I continued to learn more Spanish and observe the daily lifestyles of inmates in a Mexican prison. I remember thinking to myself one day about how much drugs and alcohol there was inside the prison. It seemed as though there were constant parties inside inmates' cells, which explained why there were frequent Revisions. There were 14 dormitories, and in each dorm there was one inmate responsible for selling cocaine. In my dorm there were two guys down the hall from me where all of the money would end up being delivered to their cell every afternoon. After the money was counted it was delivered to the big boss next door. I'll leave his name anonymous in this book so I can sleep better at night.

This inmate controlled all of the cocaine sales in the entire prison. One day he invited me to his cell to introduce himself. His entire cell was finished out in mahogany wood shelving with a big screen television in the middle. His favorite team was the Dallas Cowboys, so we had something in common. I was surprised to see that there were so many Dallas Cowboy fans in Mexico City. We talked a lot on a daily basis and I watched first-hand how everything operated. Many of the Custodios were on the take. They would come by the boss's cell every visitation day and collect the money. This was a full-time big operation within the prison. I got to know the two inmates who counted the money next door. One of them invited me into his cell one day. "Come in, guero, I have something that I want to show you," he said. "This is a picture of my new $65,000 Corvette that I just bought. I paid for it with the money that I made here in prison last year," he told me. "I made over $100,000 in here last year," he boasted.

Everything here was about money. Either you had it, or you didn't. Lucky for me, I was still able to get money from my old neighbor Ed Phinney back in Ensenada who was able to go to my house and retrieve some money that I still had hidden there.

Stephanie ended up staying in prison in Mexico for about six months before she was extradited back to the U.S. She and her family accomplished everything they wanted. She was now on her way home, and I was locked up. The judge granted her time served when she returned and she was free. I didn't want her to do any time because of the kids. Our relationship was over, and it had been for a long time. I could never get over the fact that her family had stolen money from me. Not to mention also turning me in to the authorities.

There was this guy named Paco Mercado that would come by our cell on occasion. He was the kind of guy that was always taunting other inmates. He was always saying, "Come on, let's fight, Pinche Guero." I always blew him off because I wasn't looking for trouble. I was already in enough trouble to begin with.

But one day Paco came by and started talking shit, and I'd had enough of his bullshit. I rushed out of my cell and yelled, "Come on, Puto!" We started sparring, and it didn't take long for me to realize something was wrong. I was having a hard time getting air. The reason that I couldn't breathe was because he had caught me in the ribs. My ribs were broken and it was blocking my air. I'm not ashamed to admit that I had lost the fight.

Victor helped me get to the Medical Center where they informed me that indeed my ribs were broken. Anyone who has ever experienced broken ribs knows just how painful it is. When Oscar returned to the cell later that day to find out what had happened, he told me, "Oh, I forgot to tell you not to fight with Paco because he's a former professional boxer."

"Thanks for telling me that after my ribs are broken," I said.

For the next six months it would be hard for me to get around. I couldn't sleep on my left side, and it was difficult for me to put my shoes on every day. Nevertheless, time for me here continued to move fast. I never thought that I would want time to move slowly while I'm in prison. I knew that my day of judgement was coming soon, and there was nothing that I could do about it.

After the first year I had already lost my first appeal. Now, in my second year here, I was awaiting my second appeal. Remember, Doc was arrested way back in '96, and now it was getting closer to the year 2000. Many people that were involved in my case were either finished with their incarceration, or almost at the end while I still hadn't been brought to justice. According to my attorney in the U.S., the Federal government had already built their case against me.

In the meantime, while I constantly tried to make a decision on when I should go back and face my charges, life went on in Reclusorio Oriente. Every few days I would see an inmate frantically trying to make it to the Infirmary. Most of the time they would be bleeding from a stab wound. Inmates died here on a regular basis. Most of the time it was over money and drugs. All too often someone owed money, and couldn't pay. One thing that you don't want to do is owe someone money in here. There were a lot of inmates who would get caught stealing that were also getting beat up or stabbed. If it wasn't yours or you don't have the money, then you better leave it alone! In here they don't play around with their money! Mexico City has a big problem with thieves and robberies, so the majority of inmates were incarcerated for these reasons. Not to mention, cocaine and marijuana were cheap, and in abundance in here. Cocaine was 10 dollars a gram and marijuana was one dollar a joint. Just about anything and everything you could imagine was smuggled into the prison. Oscar told me a story about a prison breakout that had happened about six months before my arrival. An inmate had a grenade smuggled into the prison. They blew a hole in the wall where five or six inmates had escaped. Several inmates were captured, and several others were killed.

And one inmate escaped. This place was crazy! Paco would

still come by and hang out with us every once in a while. I think he had some kind of respect for me because I wasn't scared to fight him like most of the inmates. I'm not sure I would have either if I had known at the time that he was a former professional boxer. Anyway, it's like they say, "it is what it is." By now I knew just about every bad Spanish word that was possible. Hence, the name Guero Chilangro. So at that point when someone talked shit to me, I could throw it right back at them.

My attorney in Mexico came to see me as I was approaching the final appeal deadline. At this point I could still agree to come back and face my charges before the final appeal. If I decided to wait until the final appeal decision then I would be brought back to the U.S. against my will, and that definitely wouldn't fare well with the Judge. After two years and nine months in a Mexican prison I decided it was time for me to drop my final appeal and return to the U.S. and face my charges. Two days later the U.S Marshals showed up at Reclusorio Oriente to pick me up. That would be my last day in a Mexican prison.

CHAPTER 43

JUDGEMENT DAY

The next thing that I know, I'm being escorted through the Mexico City airport by two U.S. Marshals. I was handcuffed with a small blanket covering my hands so I wouldn't be as noticeable to civilians. Once we were in the air the U.S. Marshal sitting next to me said, "Mr. King, I was searching for you more than ten years, and now I get to meet you."

I didn't say anything. There wasn't much that I could say.

When we finally arrived in the U.S. they escorted me through the airport in San Antonio, Texas. I ended up staying in some holdover prison in San Antonio for one night, and the next morning I was placed on a Federal bus with other inmates on a one-way ticket straight to Waco, Texas to face all of my charges in Federal Court. They held me in a county jail in Waco while I awaited my court date. I decided to use a court appointed attorney. At this point that was a good decision for several reasons. First of all, I was out of money now, and it wouldn't be so easy to raise 50,000 dollars or more for a high-dollar attorney. Second, I was informed that with this Judge it didn't matter whether or not you had an expensive attorney or a court appointed attorney. The court appointed me a former prosecutor by the name of Stanley Schweiger.

My trial would be in the courtroom of U.S. Federal Judge Walter Smith. He was known for being one of the toughest Federal Judges in the country. He was known for being tough on crime, especially on drug cases. To say that I was nervous about my court date would be an understatement. My next meeting with my attorney, he informed me that, based on the quantity of Ecstasy, along with multiple other charges, including the fugitive charge, that I could be facing anywhere from 25 years to life in prison. He also informed me, that if I tried to fight the charges that I would most certainly receive a life sentence, and that the only chance I had was to accept responsibility for all of my charges, and hope for the best. Remember, this was the same court where Judge Walter Smith had previously sentenced the Branch Davidians to 99 years each for their involvement in the David Koresh Davidian compound incident.

With my next meeting with my attorney I asked, "What's the best that I can hope for?"

"With the drug charges that you're facing, you could be looking at up to 20 years, and with the fugitive charge, you could be looking at the max of another five years. So you could be looking at up to 25 years," he told me. "That's your worst case scenario. They already feel like they have a good case against you. So, the only thing that you can really do is accept responsibility for your charges."

Then he told me, "If you fight your charges, then you could end up spending the rest of your life in prison."

"What about the time that I spent incarcerated in Mexico?" I asked.

"Because you were being held for a charge in the U.S., you will be given credit for that time on your sentence. If you would have been in prison in Mexico for charges there, then you wouldn't get credit. Anytime that you're being held somewhere on extradition charges, the time spent in another country applies," the attorney explained.

I awaited my trial date for several months in the Waco county jail. It was hard for me to sleep well. It was very stressful wondering what my future would hold for me. Nothing to do but lay in your bunk and wait for your name to be called.

The day of my trial, they escorted about eight inmates, including myself, into a van and headed to the Federal courthouse. When we arrived, they placed all of us in a holding cell together, and began calling one inmate at a time to be escorted to the courtroom. I sat and watched each inmate return from court one at a time. Most of the guys came back to the holding cell with a sad look on their face, and some were even in tears for getting a five-year sentence. I wished that I was only getting a five-year sentence, I thought to myself.

All of the anxiety and anticipation was now over. The guard called my name, and I was now being escorted to the courtroom. The courtroom was full of people. They were all standing, and looking back at me as I entered the room. I didn't see anyone that I knew except for my attorney who was waiting for me. Here I was standing in front of the judge with my attorney. "Mr. King, how do you plead?" the judge asked.

"Guilty, Your Honor," I replied.

"Ok, Mr. King, for the drug charges I'm sentencing you to 130 months in Federal prison, and for the fugitive charge, I'm sentencing you to an additional 50 months for a total of 180 months, or 15 years total," the judge declared.

My attorney turned to me and whispered, "You got a good deal."

Immediately, the prosecutor stood up and said, "Judge, you should give this man more time."

"My decision is final," the judge said.

Although 15 years is a long time, I knew that I was guilty, and I was prepared to serve my time. I knew that someday I would get another chance at freedom, and that's all I could ask for. After my return to the holding cell, shortly afterwards we were escorted back to the van and driven back to the county jail. The other inmates kept looking at me to see what my expression was. "How much time did they give you?" one inmate asked.

"15 years," I replied.

Nobody said anything. Everyone kept staring at me to see what my expression was. "You don't look very upset for someone who was just sentenced to 15 years in prison," one of the inmates said.

"Although 15 years is a long time, I'm just happy that I'll get another chance at freedom someday," I told him.

We all were returned to our holding cells in the county jail where we would wait to see which Federal Correctional Institution we would be sent to. Several weeks later I was informed that I would be going to F.C.I. Texarkana. I had several more days to sit and wait for my name to be called. I boarded a Federal bus with other inmates, and just like that I was on my way. For the most part, it was just like you see in the movies where you see inmates riding on a bus on their way to prison. We all wore orange jumpsuits, and were chained and handcuffed to each other. Nevertheless, I knew wherever I ended up that it was a chance for me to start over again.

Being handcuffed and shackled to other inmates on a Federal prison bus was not my idea of a good time. But after being a fugitive for almost ten years, it seemed as though the weight of the world was now off my shoulders. I had already prepared myself mentally to make the best of my situation. Just knowing that someday I would get another chance at freedom made my ride to prison a little bit easier. When we finally arrived at F.C.I. Texarkana, the first thing after processing us was to lead me to a big open dormitory with bunks and inmates everywhere. The first thing that I noticed were inmates in tank tops with big muscles everywhere. *These guys must live and breathe the weight pile. I want to look like these guys someday,* I thought to myself. I never had really worked out that much growing up. When I first looked at myself in a big mirror in the bathroom, I remember how bad I looked. I looked like someone who had been using drugs for years, and didn't take good care of my body. With that one look at myself in the mirror that day, I made a promise to myself to change everything in my life from that point on. I wanted to come out of here a different man. I wanted to re-invent myself. I soon learned that not every Federal prison had weights or gyms.

In prison they refer to them as weight piles. F.C.I. Texarkana just happened to be one of the prisons that still had weights. According to my understanding from other inmates, the Feds were phasing out weights in federal prisons because the inmates were getting too big. Once the weights were destroyed, then they were not going to be replaced. So all inmates who worked out kept a close eye on anyone who wasn't taking care of them. You didn't want to make these guys mad! Not only did F.C.I. Texarkana have weights, but they had two weight piles on the yard. It didn't take long for me to settle into my new surroundings. I studied other inmate's workouts, and read about proper diet and exercise. For someone like myself, it took the next several years before I began seeing a transformation in my body. I went from someone with no muscles to someone with muscles and a six-pack to go with it. The old phrase "you are what you eat," could never be more true. I read just about every book written on abdominal exercises. After about four years of constant training and dieting I had completely transformed my body. I remember other inmates would come up to me sometimes and say something like, "I don't know what you're doing, but whatever it is that you're doing is working." Even with all of my changes, there were other guys who had been there a lot longer than me, who had better physiques than mine.

The first thing that I would share with other inmates when they came to me about training abs were the three rules, as I called them. If you're training for abs the first thing is your diet. Second, you need the proper exercise routines, and last but not least, you need to follow up the exercise routine with at least 30 to 45 minutes of cardio. A lot of guys liked to skip the cardio at the end of the workout. Maybe because it's not easy to jog or ride a bike after doing abdominal crunches or leg lifts for an hour. But for me that was the finishing point for obtaining abs. The only way to really burn fat is by doing cardio. It's hard to train for mass and abs at the same time. My only answer to that would be to train some months for mass and change your workout every few months and concentrate more on your abs. But continue to eat healthy and do some sort of abs on a daily basis. When it came to gaining mass, Arnold Schwarzenegger was the greatest ever at shocking the muscles into growing. He was the Master of the gym. He always kept the muscles guessing. Anyone interested in weightlifting should check out Arnold's videos if you haven't already. The next thing for me in my transformation was my receding hairline. I decided to shave my head. I only wish that I would have done it sooner.

I was hanging on to something that wasn't there anymore. Once you lose most of your hair, it's a lot easier to just shave your head. It looks cleaner, and actually I would find out later when I'm free one day that women actually like a cleaner look. Enough about exercise, and what I looked like in prison. I knew the path to freedom for me would be to stay out of trouble while being locked up. I couldn't afford to lose any good-time that was awarded for good behavior, or risk staying incarcerated longer than my sentence. I had to be on my best behavior. I made it a point to stay away from anything that might jeopardize my release date. I needed to be a model inmate if I wanted to be released from prison at the age of 46. I knew that the path to freedom for me would take 11 and a half years in prison. Almost three years in a Mexican prison, and eight and a half in the U.S. I could only get to 11 and a half with time off for good behavior, and a one year reduction for taking the drug program. I continued with my time at F.C.I. Texarkana for almost seven years. I continued to exercise and prepare myself mentally for my freedom someday. I knew that I would have to find a job once released from prison, but I didn't have any idea about what it would be.

The only real job that I ever had was working for myself when I owned my own restaurant. I was only in my twenties then. I had never worked for anyone else my entire life, so I didn't have a clue what I would do for work, or where I would end up. I only remember one thing that my dad had told me one time, and that was, "If you really want to work, you can always find work." I probably should have taken that advice younger in life, but I was stubborn and determined to do things my way. When you're young you think that you know everything. Nevertheless, with all of this constantly on my mind, I continued to stay focused, and concentrate on finishing my time in prison. When it finally got down to only having one year left in prison, I was transferred to F.C.I. Fort Worth in order to take the Drug Program. Upon completion of the Drug Program, I was finally released from Federal prison in June of 2009. I remember having a guard walk me to the front gate, the front gate opening, and the guard saying, "You're free to go." It had been a long time since I'd last stood on U.S. soil as a free man.

CHAPTER 45

A PRICE ON FREEDOM

Several questions that I always get are, "Was it all worth it?" Or, "Did you hide any money anywhere?" The fact that I had absolutely nothing to my name when I left prison, I would definitely say "no," it wasn't worth it. I suppose that I could have had a better plan to have some money, but the fact is I didn't. Besides, the Feds have ways of finding just about anything these days. Now that I'm older I have a much different perspective on life. It's hard to be objective about right and wrong when I was in my twenties and people were handing me millions of dollars. I can tell you from my own experience, that you can never put a price on your freedom. It's something you never realize until you lose it. When you're free you can always work to make something good happen, but when you're behind bars there's not much you can do. All of my so-called friends that wanted to hang out with me when I had everything are long gone today. I think back to one of the best times in my life, and believe it or not, it wasn't when I had millions of dollars. It was right before I was introduced to Ecstasy when I had my own restaurant. There was something about honestly earning my money from that restaurant. I appreciated it more because I worked for it.

There was never really any appreciation for the money from drug proceeds. It was always easy come, easy go. There was never any loyalty in the drug business. It was always each man for himself, and when someone messed up down the line, you had to worry about someone ratting you out. There were plenty of those to go around. When I was first introduced to Ecstasy, I had a good

136

life. I was a young 20 year old with my own restaurant. I was lured in by the thought of all the money. I used to watch "Miami Vice" in those days, where they glorified drug dealers by showing them with lots of money, fast cars and sexy ladies. All I'm saying is, be careful what you ask for because if you really pursue something and you obtain it, then that becomes part of your life, and you might find yourself in a position like myself where it was too late to turn back. There are so many legal ways to make money these days. Look for those opportunities and be ready. Either you will find them or they will find you. You'll never have to be looking over your shoulder like I did, or wondering if that would be the day that they kick your door in and you lose everything. If I would have put the same effort into making honest money, then I would have been a lot better off in the long run.

CHAPTER 46

FINAL THOUGHTS

Along the way I tried different drugs through the years. I never really got into marijuana because it always made me feel slow, stupid, and hungry. Cocaine made me feel paranoid and unsocial. Meth made me stay up for days and start multiple projects that I never would finish. The difference between Ecstasy and other drugs was that it made you sociable. Ecstasy made you feel good about everything around you. Ecstasy was a mind-opening drug that you could take with your companion or friends and sit and talk about the good things in life. That's why Ecstasy is referred to as the "Love Drug".

As I'm finishing this book here during these tough times in America with the coronavirus pandemic, I would like to report some recent good news for our military veterans who suffer from Post-Traumatic Stress Disorder (PTSD). Recently, the FDA has granted expanded access for treatments using the drug "Ecstasy," or MDMA. There are clinical trials ongoing in the United States, Canada, and Israel which are scheduled for completion in 2021, and the FDA could finally approve the treatment in 2022. I'm surprised that it hasn't happened sooner since Ecstasy helps the mind, body, and spirit all come together as one.

As for me, I moved to San Diego, California after my release from prison. I slept on my brother's sofa since I had nothing to my name. I found work at the local shipyards where I still work to this day.

The purpose of me writing this book was never intended to glorify my past, but to simply share my crazy, unorthodox journey to where I am today. I'm not crying over "spilled milk". I did the crime, and I did the time. Be careful what you wish for, especially when you're young. If I can give any advice it would be, make good decisions, work hard, and enjoy life. Life is too short to lose time. On a sad note, Jimmy was hit and killed along with a female accomplice while attempting to elude police after fleeing from a routine stop in Denton, Texas on Thursday, January 24th, 2013.

I would like to thank writer and editor Michael Valentino for his patience, hard work, and dedication to help me bring this story to fruition. I would like to thank my brother Justin along with my co-workers Danny, Rolando, Jeovany, and Omar for inspiring me to write this book. I would also like to thank writer and producer Richard Stratton for inspiring me to keep writing.